Trust in the Lord with
All your heart
And lean not on your
own understanding;
In all your ways submit
to him
And he will make your
paths straight

Proverbs 3:5-6

Printed by CreateSpace, An Amazon.com Company

Belong's to Evianne

Date: _____

My Requests:

Bible Verse:

My Prayer:

Answers:

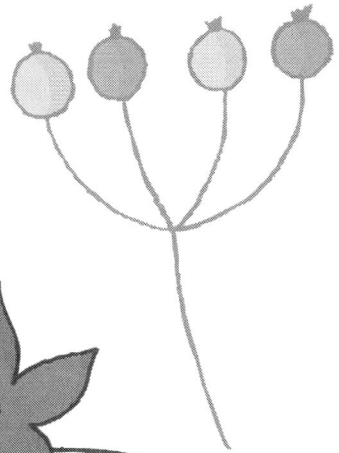

Thank You, Lord For...

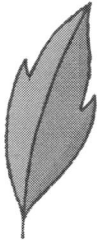

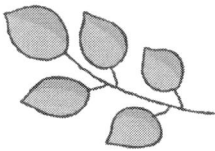

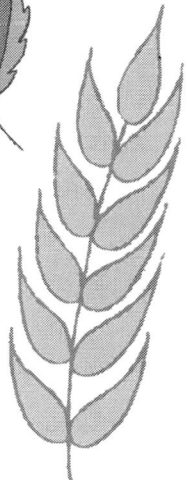

Date: _____

My Requests:

Bible Verse:

My Prayer:

Answers:

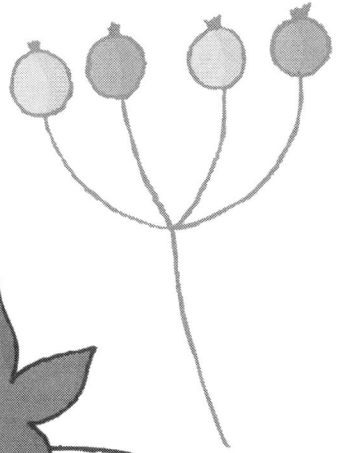

Thank You, Lord For...

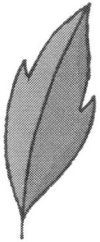

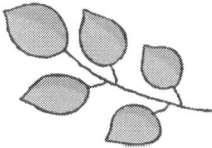

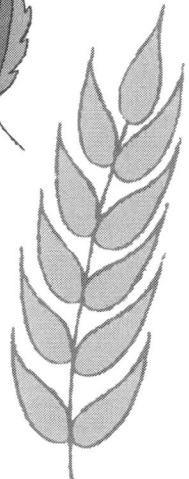

Date: _____

My Requests:

Bible Verse:

My Prayer:

Answers:

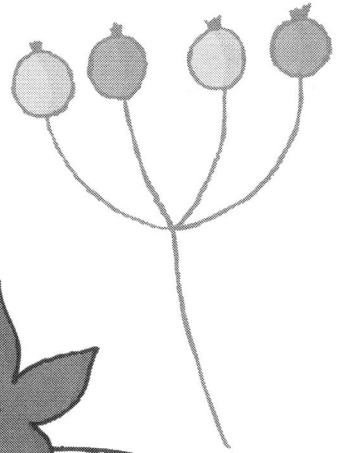

Thank You, Lord For...

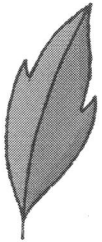

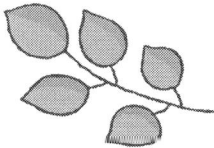

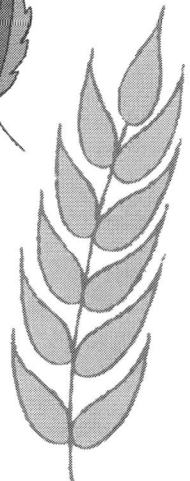

Date: _____

My Requests:

Bible Verse:

My Prayer:

Answers:

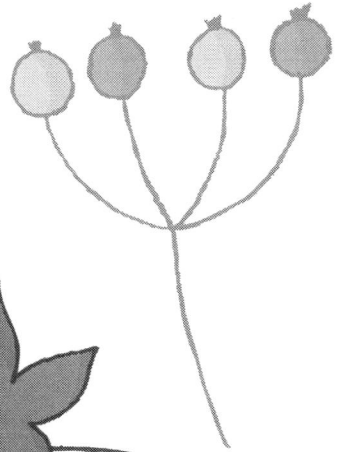

Thank You, Lord For...

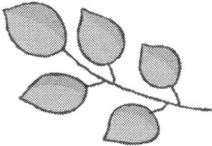

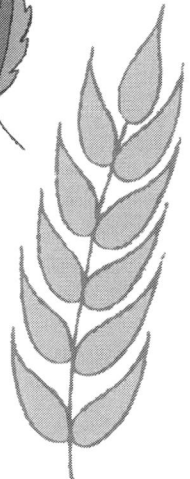

Date: _____

My Requests:

Bible Verse:

My Prayer:

Answers:

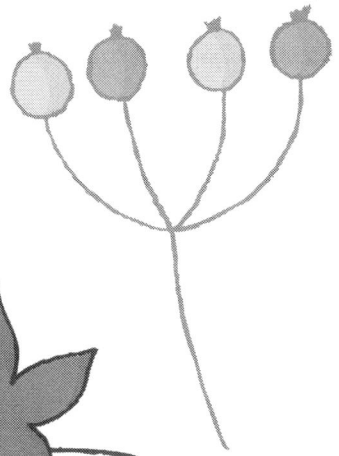

Thank You, Lord For...

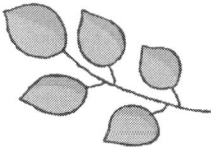

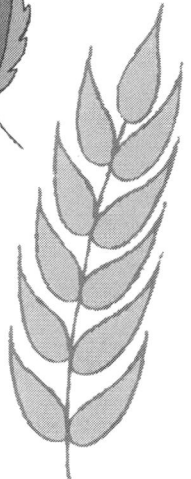

Date: _____

My Requests:

Bible Verse:

My Prayer:

Answers:

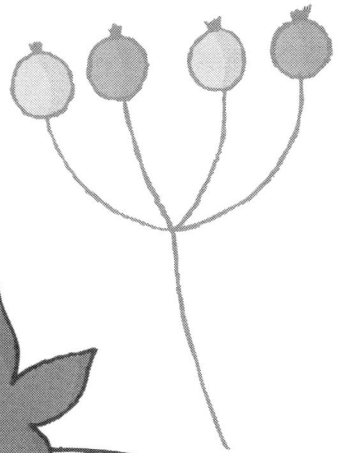

Thank You, Lord For...

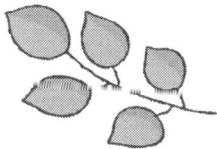

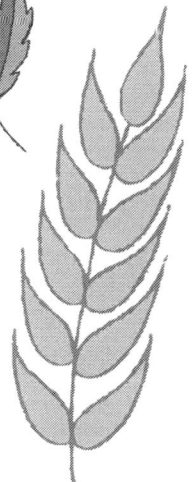

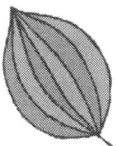

Date: _____

My Requests:

Bible Verse:

My Prayer:

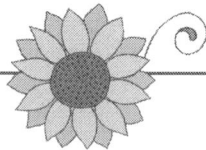

Answers:

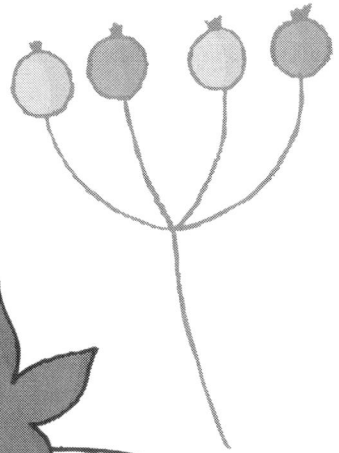

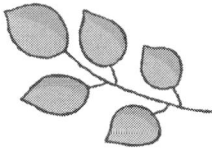

Thank You, Lord For...

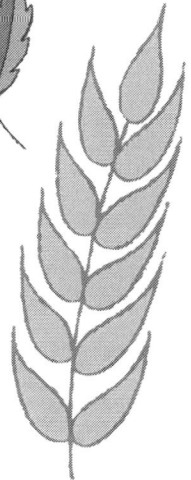

Date: _____

My Requests:

Bible Verse:

My Prayer:

Answers:

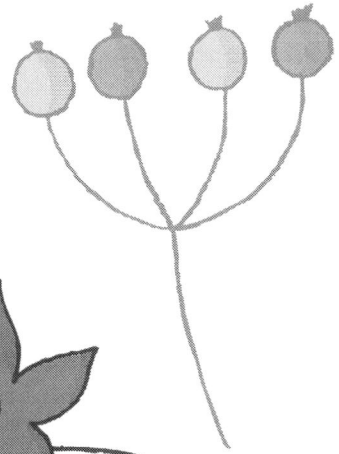

Thank You, Lord For...

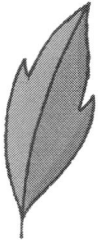

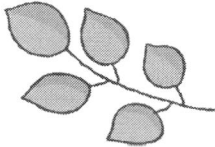

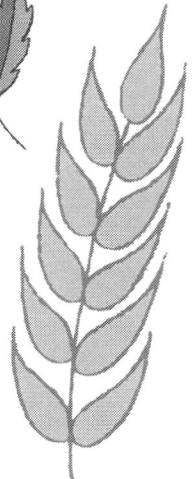

Date: _____

My Requests:

Bible Verse:

My Prayer:

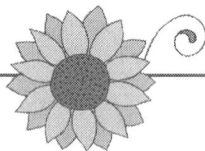

Answers:

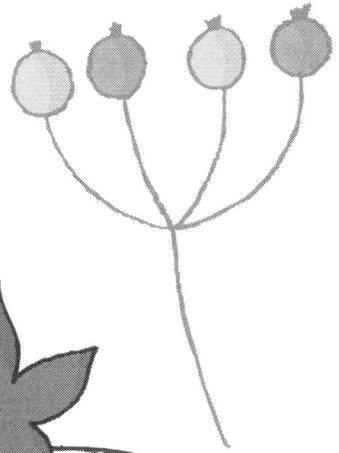

Thank You, Lord For...

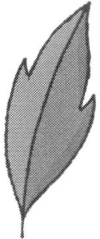

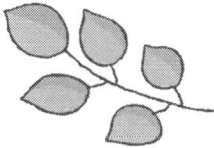

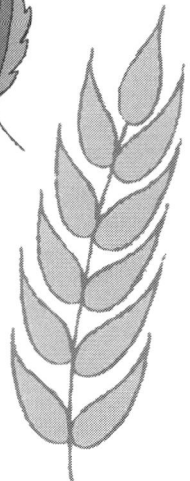

Date: _____

My Requests:

Bible Verse:

My Prayer:

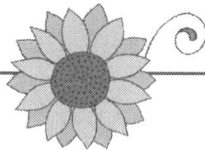

Answers:

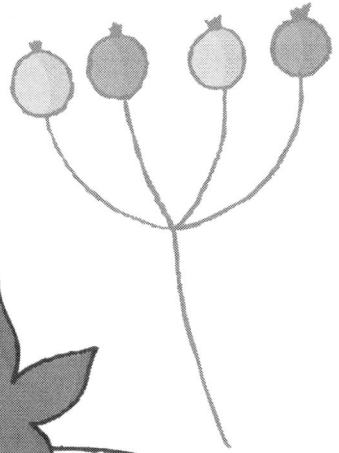

Thank You, Lord For...

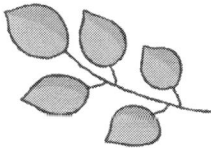

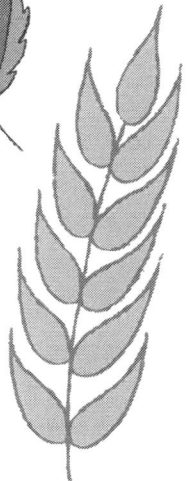

Date: _____

My Requests:

Bible Verse:

My Prayer:

Answers:

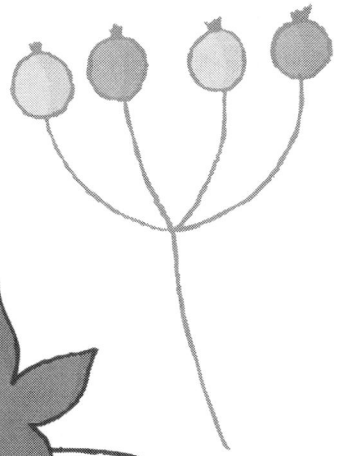

Thank You, Lord For...

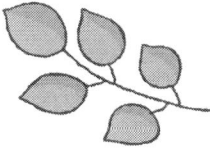

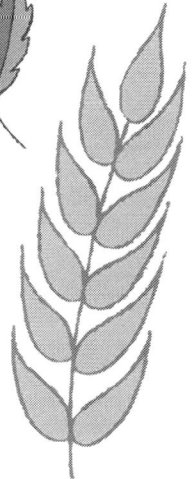

Date: _____

My Requests:

Bible Verse:

My Prayer:

Answers:

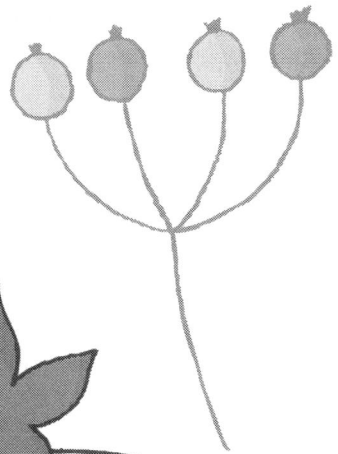

Thank You, Lord For...

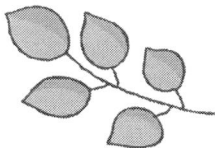

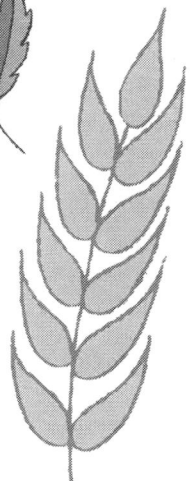

Date: _____

My Requests:

Bible Verse:

My Prayer:

Answers:

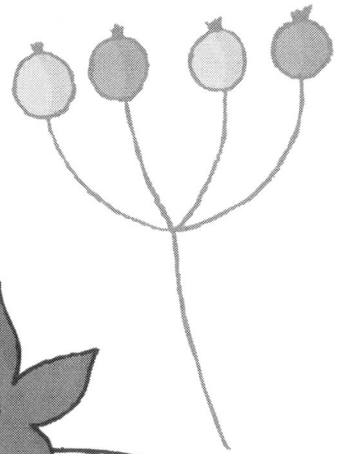

Thank You, Lord For...

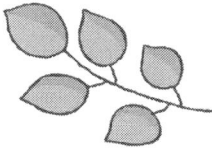

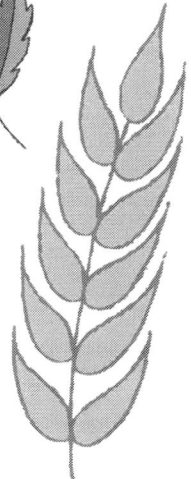

Date: _____

My Requests:

Bible Verse:

My Prayer:

Answers:

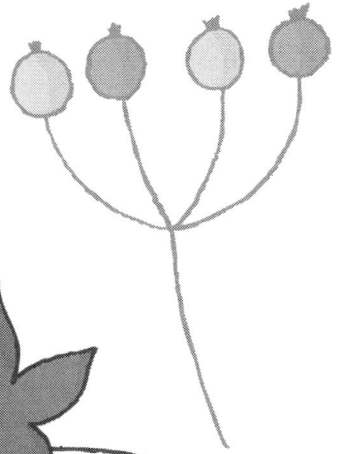

Thank You, Lord For...

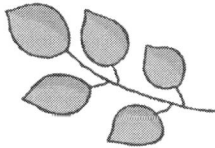

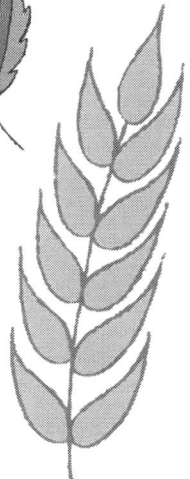

Date: _____

My Requests:

Bible Verse:

My Prayer:

Answers:

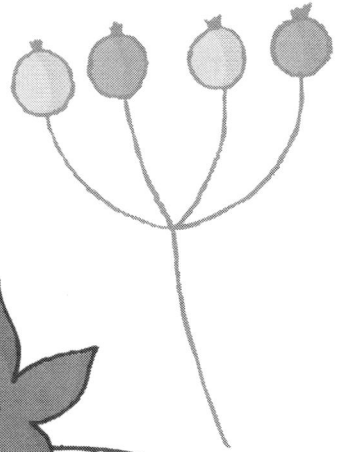

Thank You, Lord For...

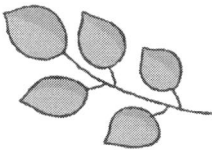

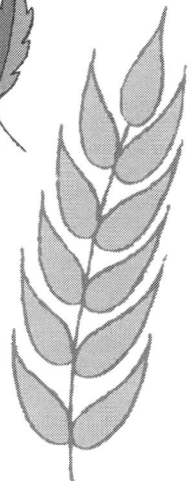

Date: _____

My Requests:

Bible Verse:

My Prayer:

Answers:

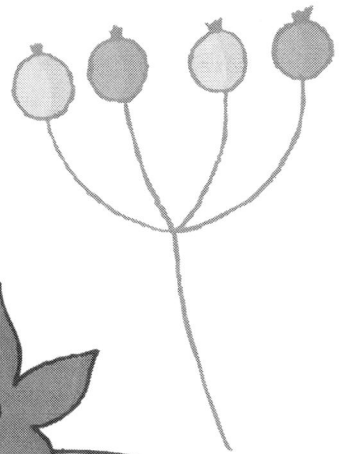

Thank You, Lord For...

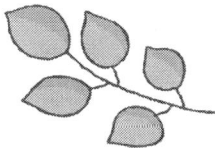

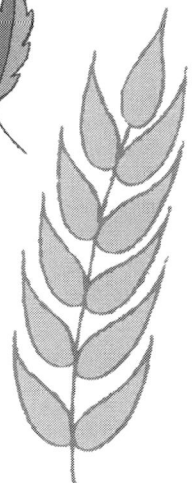

Date: _____

My Requests:

Bible Verse:

My Prayer:

Answers:

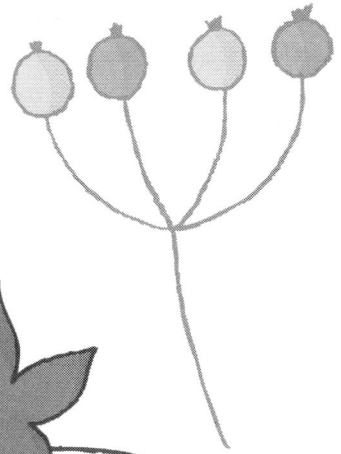

Thank You, Lord For...

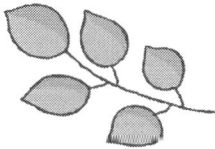

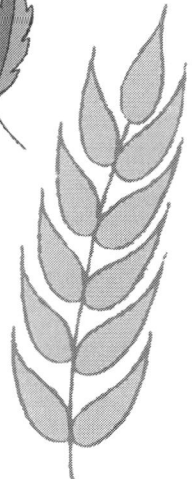

Date: _____

My Requests:

Bible Verse:

My Prayer:

Answers:

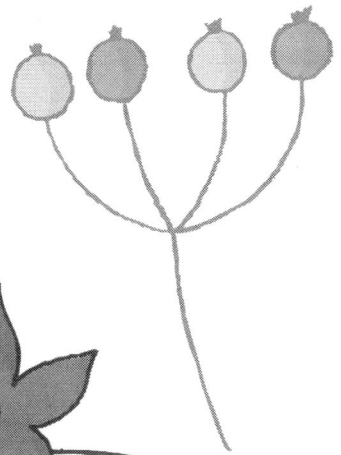

Thank You, Lord For...

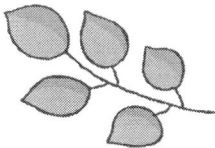

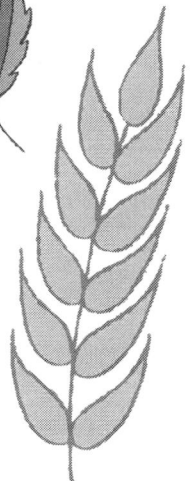

Date: _____

My Requests:

Bible Verse:

My Prayer:

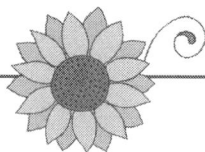

Answers:

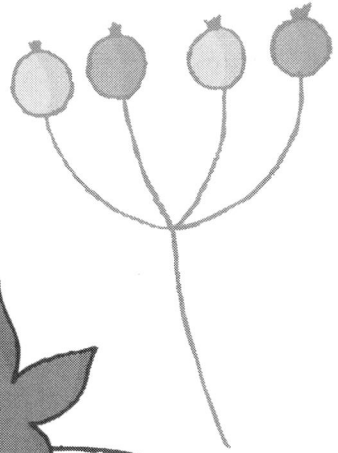

Thank You, Lord For...

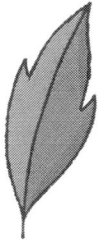

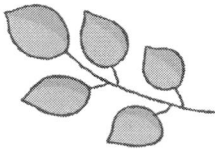

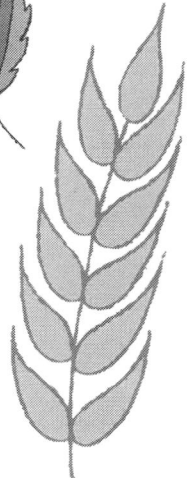

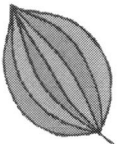

Date: _____

My Requests:

Bible Verse:

My Prayer:

Answers:

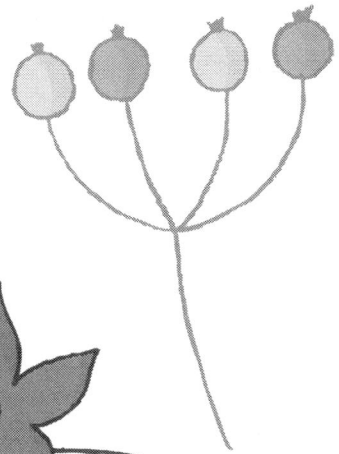

Thank You, Lord For...

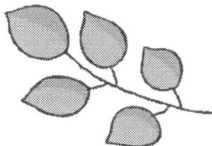

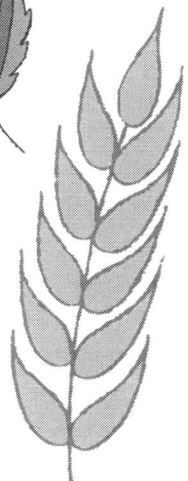

Date: _____

My Requests:

Bible Verse:

My Prayer:

Answers:

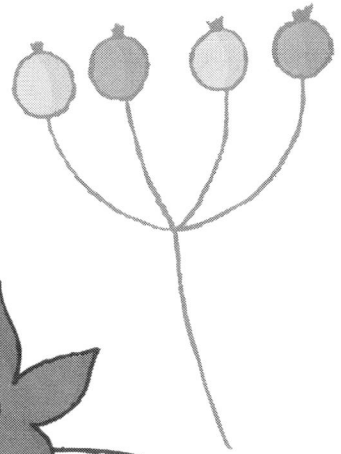

Thank You, Lord For...

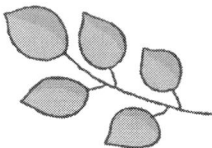

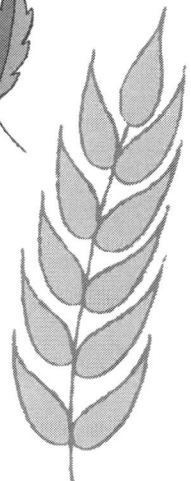

Date: _____

My Requests:

Bible Verse:

My Prayer:

Answers:

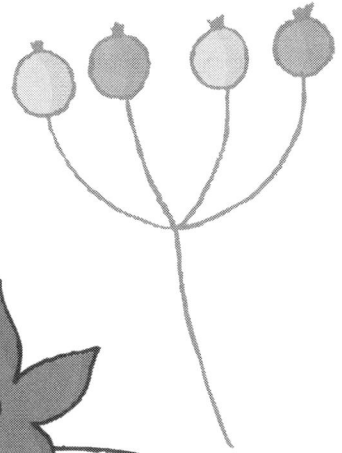

Thank You, Lord For...

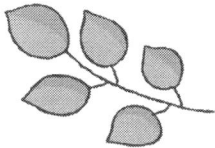

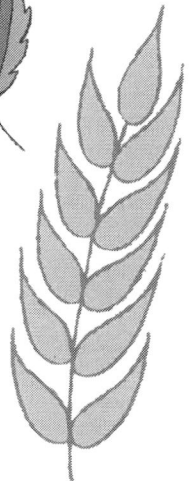

Date: _____

My Requests:

Bible Verse:

My Prayer:

Answers:

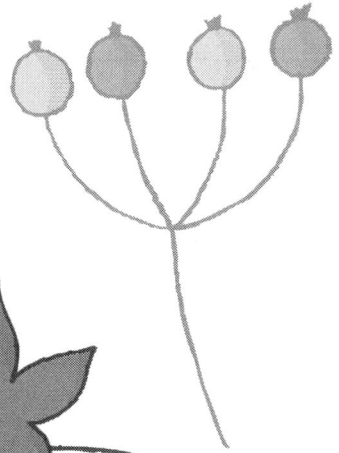

Thank You, Lord For...

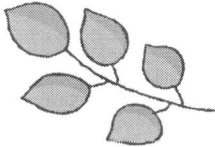

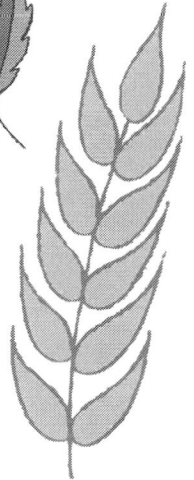

Date: _____

My Requests:

Bible Verse:

My Prayer:

Answers:

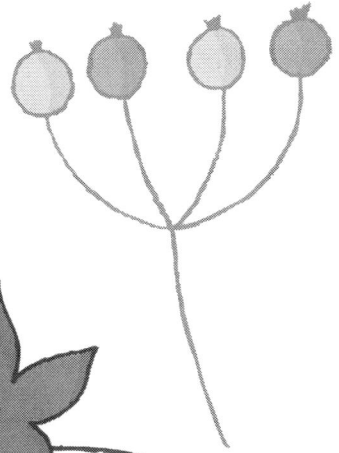

Thank You, Lord For...

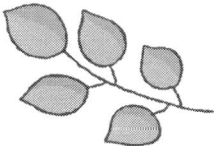

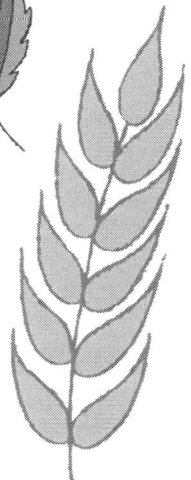

Date: _____

My Requests:

Bible Verse:

My Prayer:

Answers:

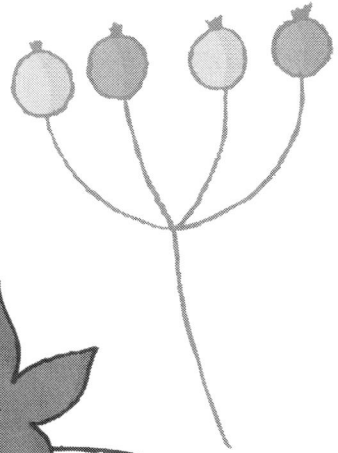

Thank You, Lord For...

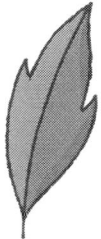

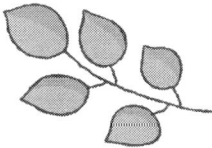

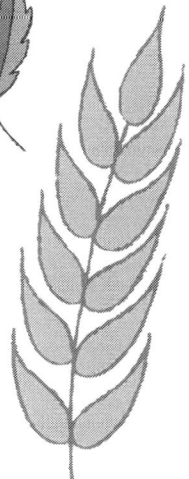

Date: _____

My Requests:

Bible Verse:

My Prayer:

Answers:

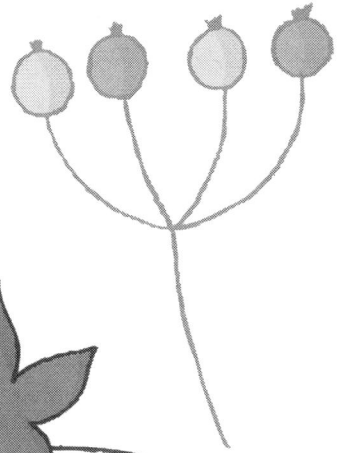

Thank You, Lord For...

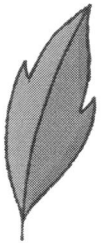

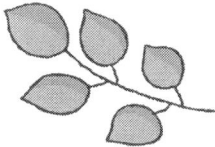

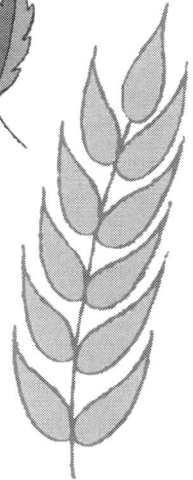

Date: _____

My Requests:

Bible Verse:

My Prayer:

Answers:

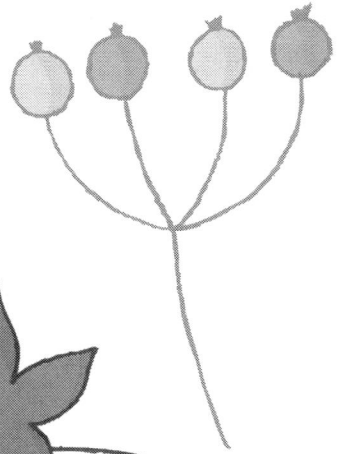

Thank You, Lord For...

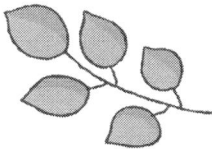

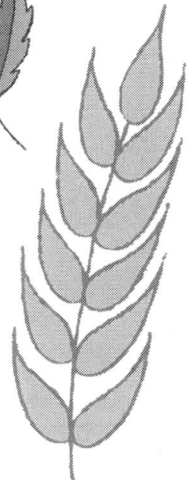

Date: _____

My Requests:

Bible Verse:

My Prayer:

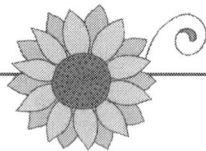

Answers:

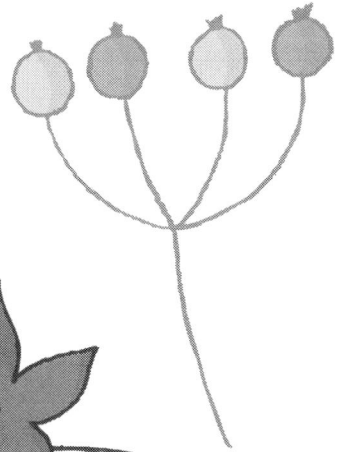

Thank You, Lord For...

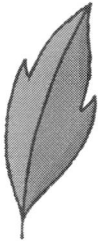

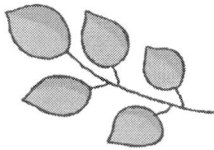

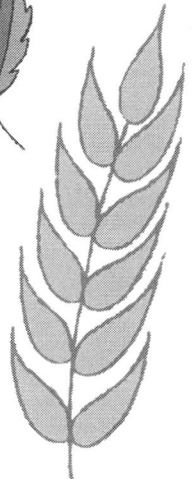

Date: _____

My Requests:

Bible Verse:

My Prayer:

Answers:

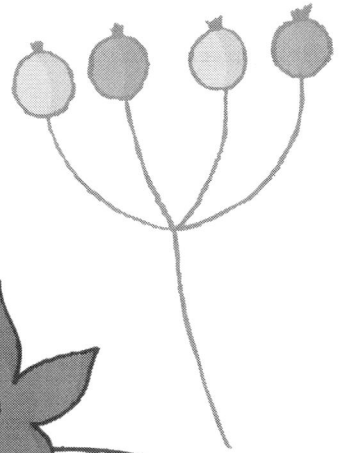

Thank You, Lord For...

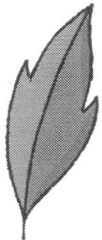

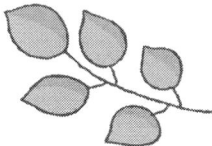

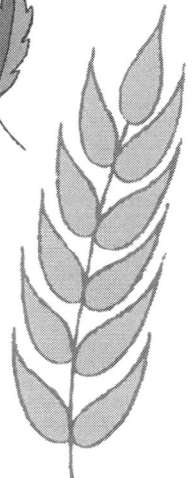

Date: _____

My Requests:

Bible Verse:

My Prayer:

Answers:

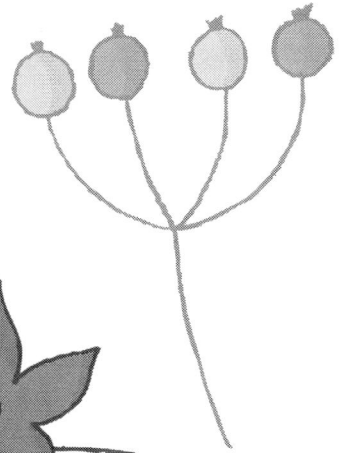

Thank You, Lord For...

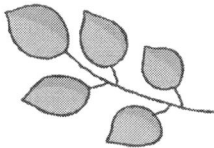

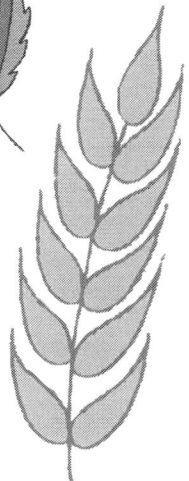

Date: _____

My Requests:

Bible Verse:

My Prayer:

Answers:

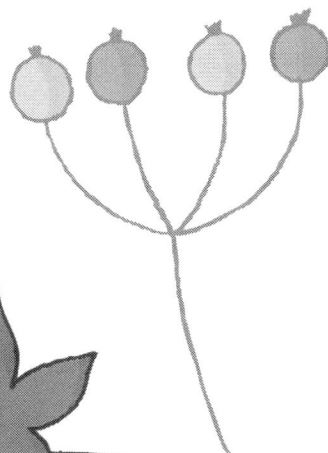

Thank You, Lord For...

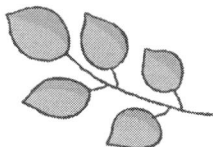

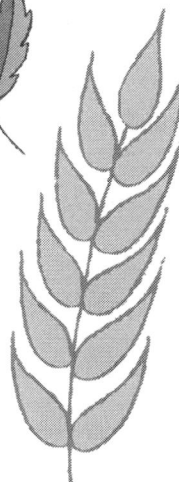

Date: _____

My Requests:

Bible Verse:

My Prayer:

Answers:

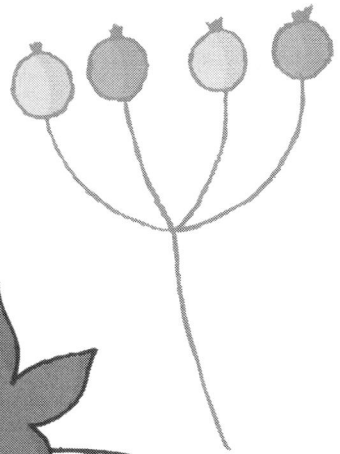

Thank You, Lord For...

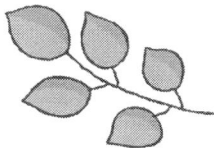

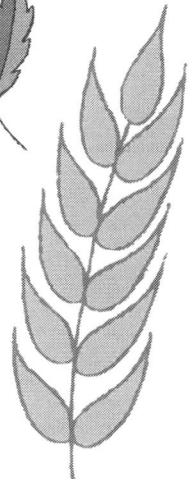

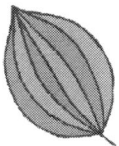

Date: _____

My Requests:

Bible Verse:

My Prayer:

Answers:

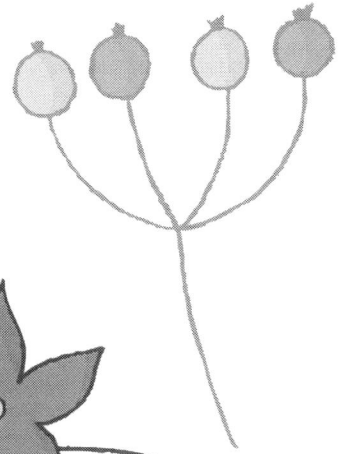

Thank You, Lord For...

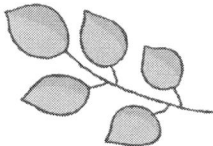

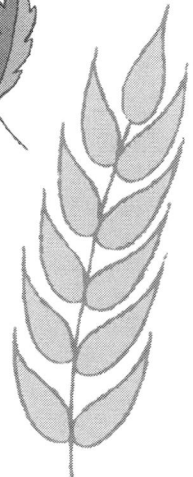

Date: _____

My Requests:

Bible Verse:

My Prayer:

Answers:

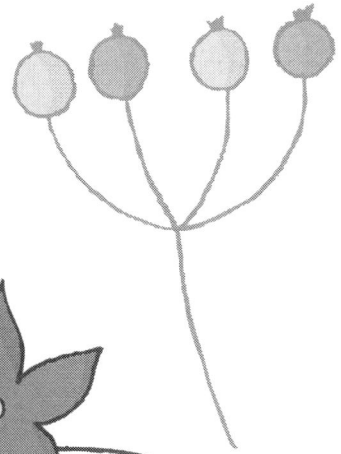

Thank You, Lord For...

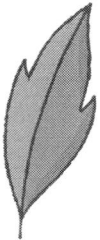

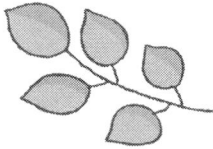

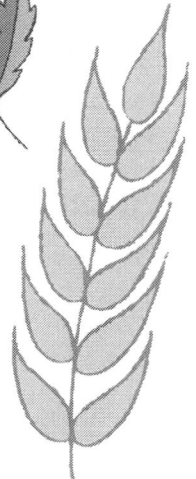

Date: _____

My Requests:

Bible Verse:

My Prayer:

Answers:

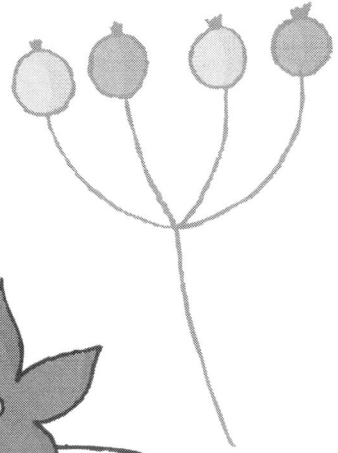

Thank You, Lord For...

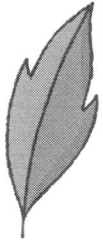
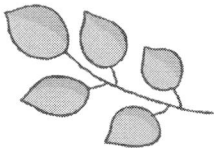

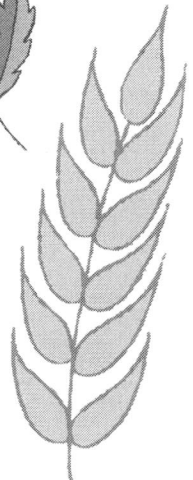

Date: _____

My Requests:

Bible Verse:

My Prayer:

Answers:

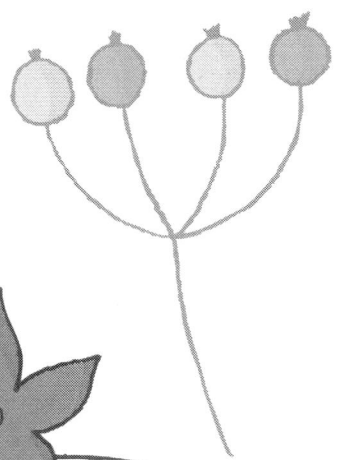

Thank You, Lord For...

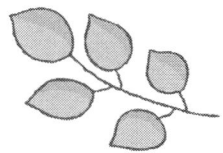

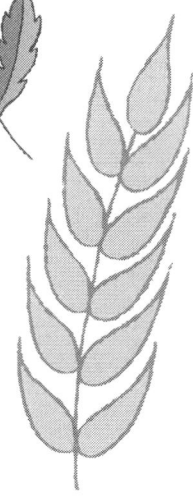

Date: _____

My Requests:

Bible Verse:

My Prayer:

Answers:

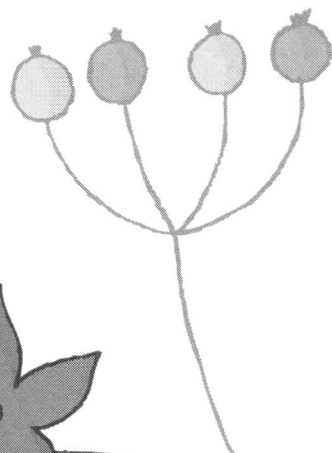

Thank You, Lord For...

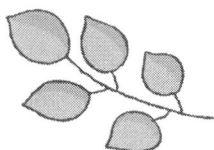

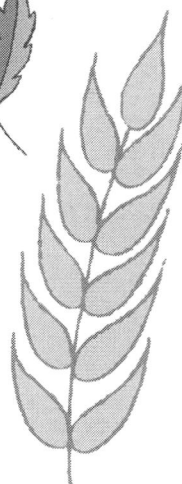

Date: _____

My Requests:

Bible Verse:

My Prayer:

Answers:

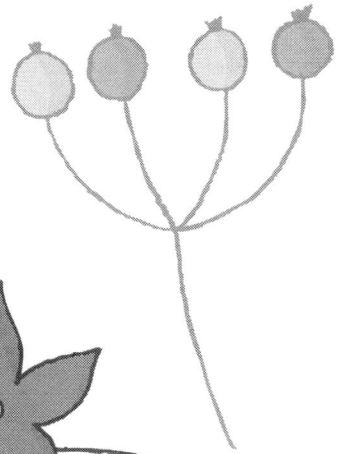

Thank You, Lord For...

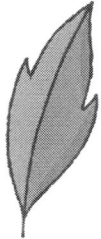
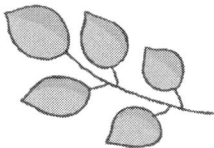

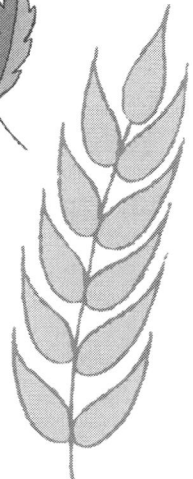

Date: _____

My Requests:

Bible Verse:

My Prayer:

Answers:

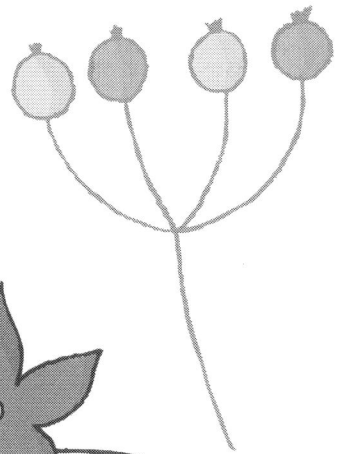

Thank You, Lord For...

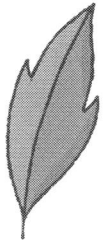

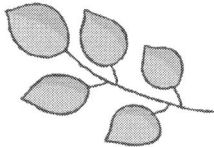

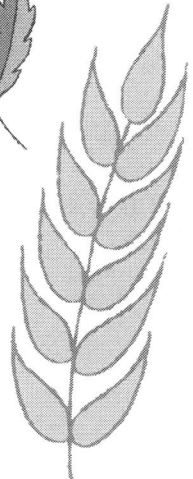

Date: _____

My Requests:

Bible Verse:

My Prayer:

Answers:

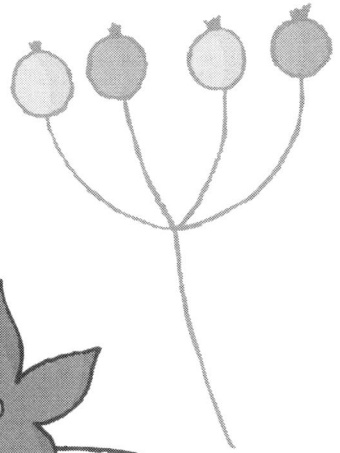

Thank You, Lord For...

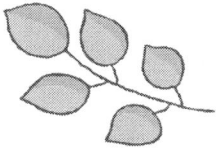

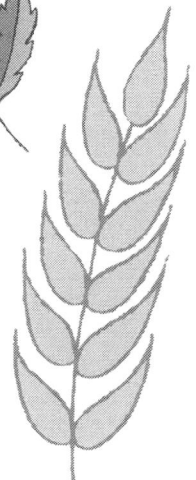

Date: _____

My Requests:

Bible Verse:

My Prayer:

Answers:

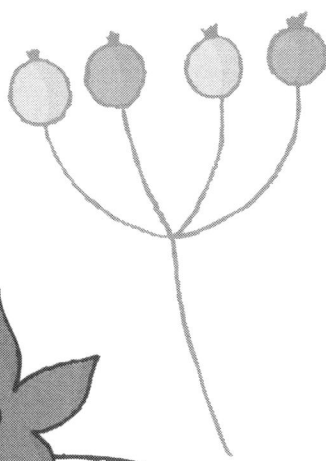

Thank You, Lord For...

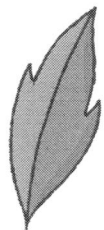

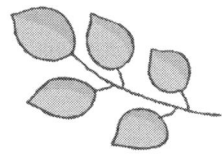

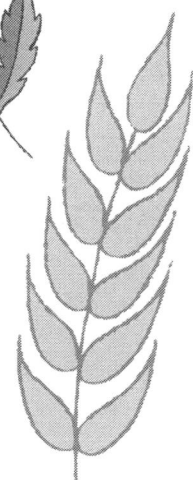

Date: _____

My Requests:

Bible Verse:

My Prayer:

Answers:

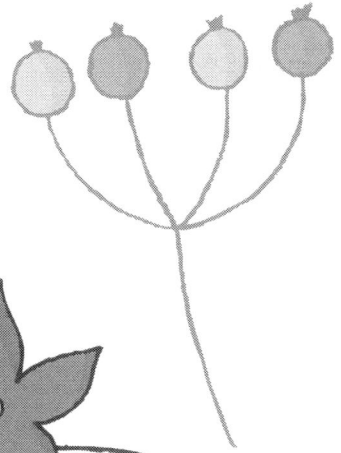

Thank You, Lord For...

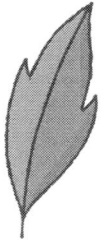

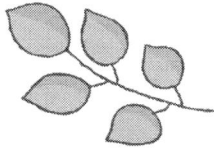

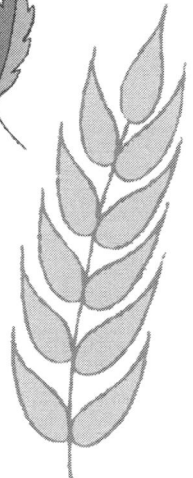

Date: _____

My Requests:

Bible Verse:

My Prayer:

Answers:

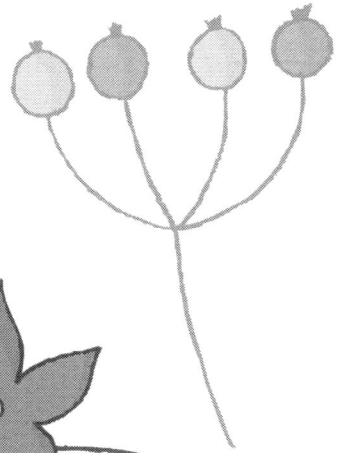

Thank You, Lord For...

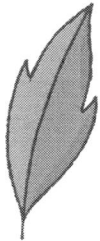
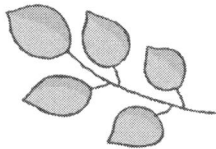

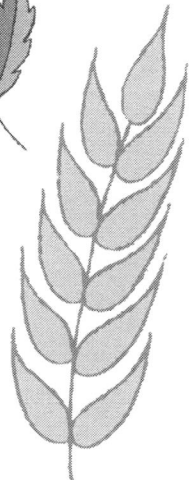

Date: _____

My Requests:

Bible Verse:

My Prayer:

Answers:

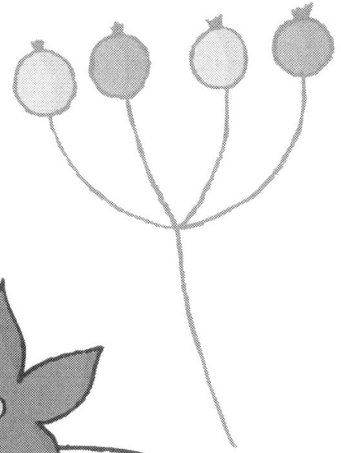

Thank You, Lord For...

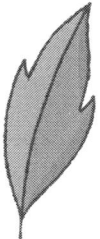

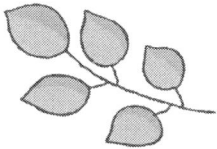

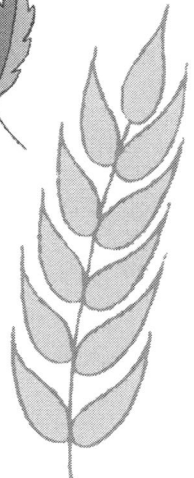

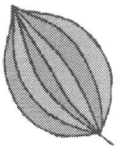

Date: _____

My Requests:

Bible Verse:

My Prayer:

Answers:

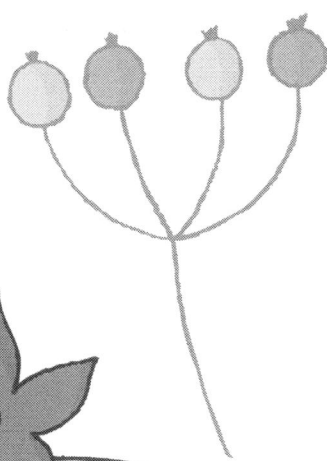

Thank You, Lord For...

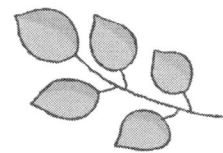

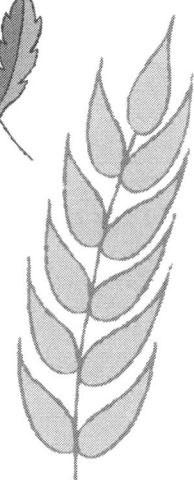

Date: _____

My Requests:

Bible Verse:

My Prayer:

Answers:

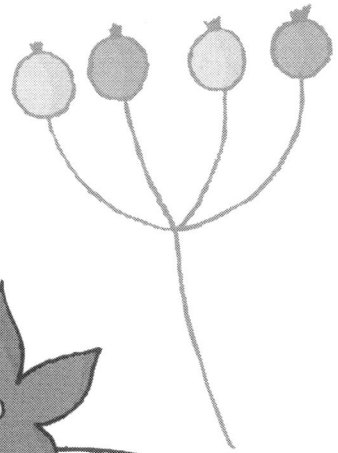

Thank You, Lord For...

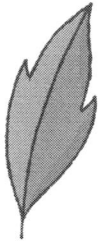
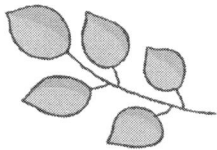

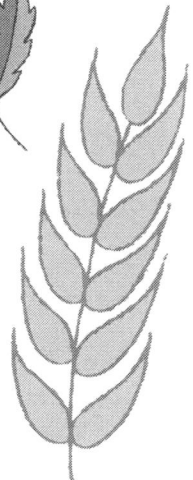

Date: _____

My Requests:

Bible Verse:

My Prayer:

Answers:

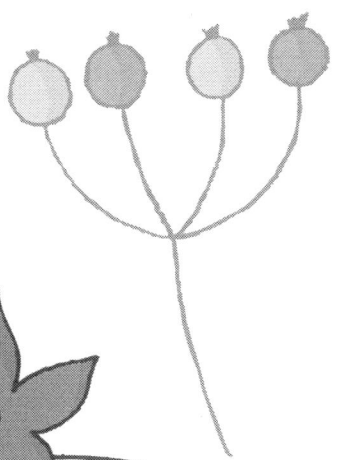

Thank You, Lord For...

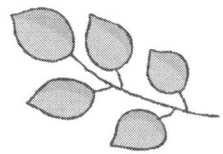

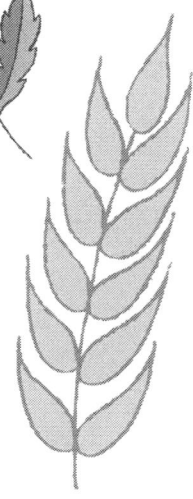

Date: _____

My Requests:

Bible Verse:

My Prayer:

Answers:

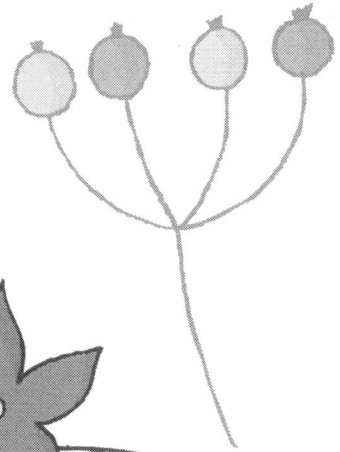

Thank You, Lord For...

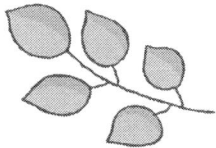

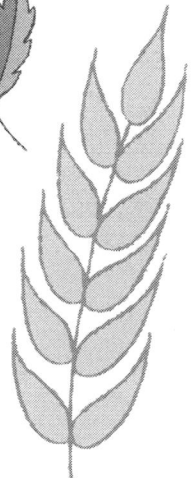

Date: _____

My Requests:

Bible Verse:

My Prayer:

Answers:

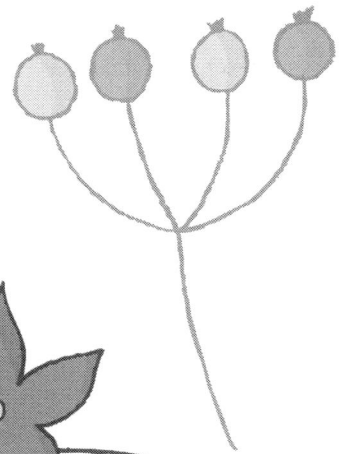

Thank You, Lord For...

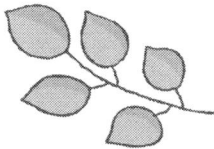

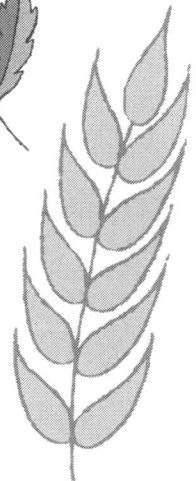

Date: _____

My Requests:

Bible Verse:

My Prayer:

Answers:

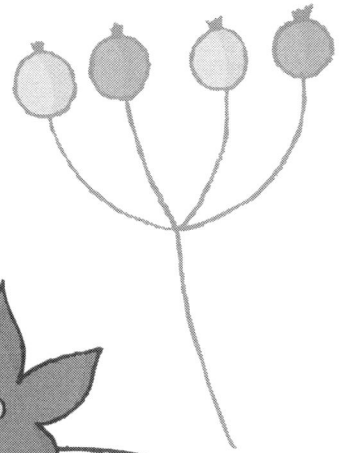

Thank You, Lord For...

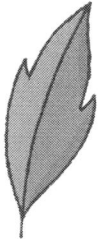

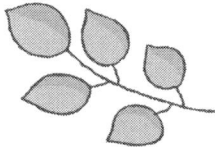

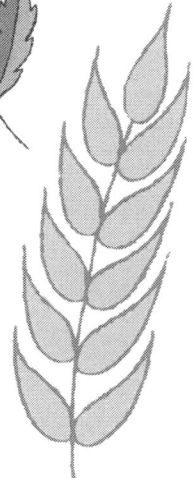

Date: _____

My Requests:

Bible Verse:

My Prayer:

Answers:

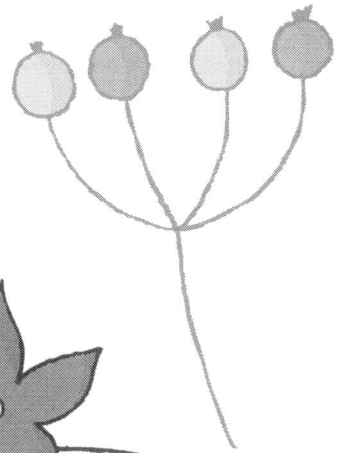

Thank You, Lord For...

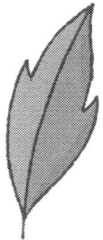

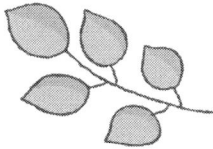

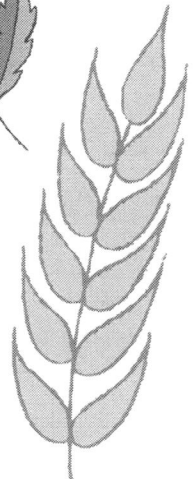

Date: _____

My Requests:

Bible Verse:

My Prayer:

Answers:

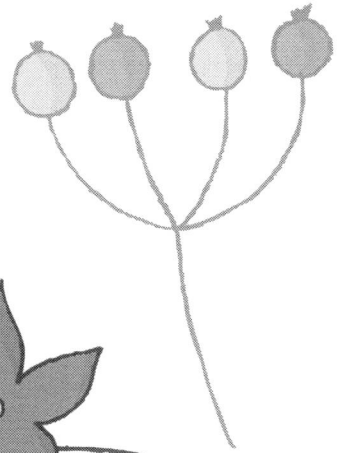

Thank You, Lord For...

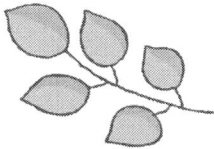

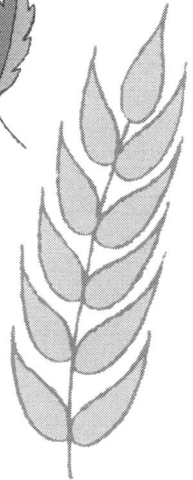

Date: _____

My Requests:

Bible Verse:

My Prayer:

Answers:

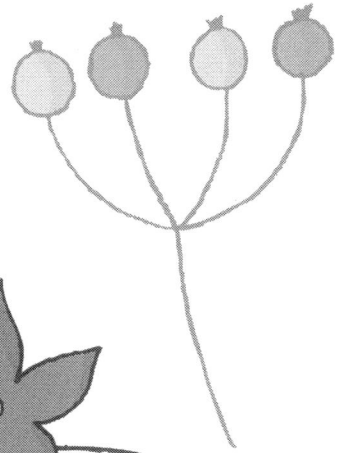

Thank You, Lord For...

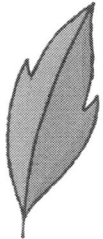

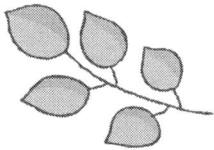

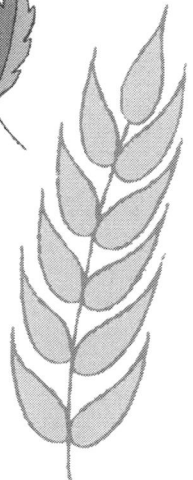

Date: _____

My Requests:

Bible Verse:

My Prayer:

Answers:

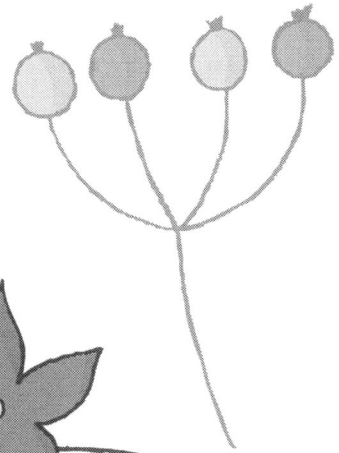

Thank You, Lord For...

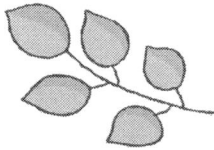

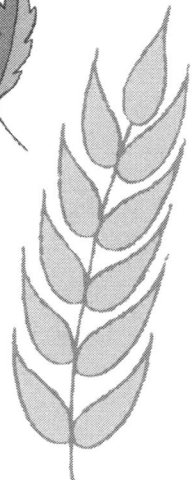

Date: _____

My Requests:

Bible Verse:

My Prayer:

Answers:

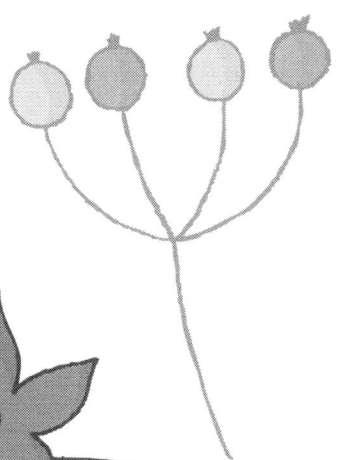

Thank You, Lord For...

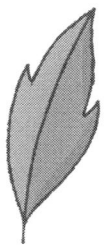

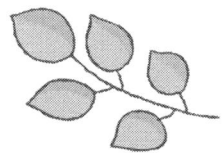

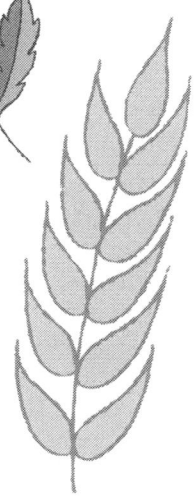

Date: _____

My Requests:

Bible Verse:

My Prayer:

Answers:

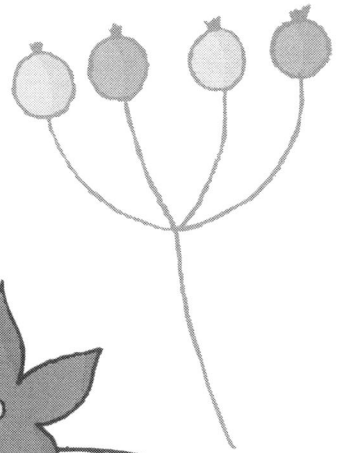

Thank You, Lord For...

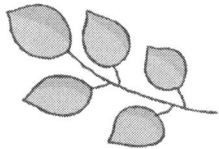

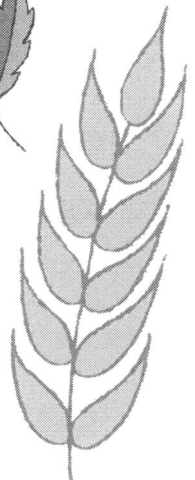

Date: _____

My Requests:

Bible Verse:

My Prayer:

Answers:

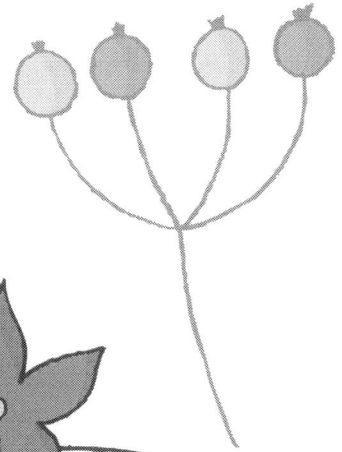

Thank You, Lord For...

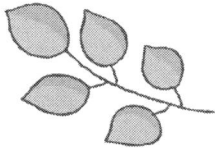

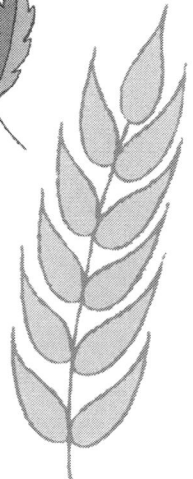

Date: _____

My Requests:

Bible Verse:

My Prayer:

Answers:

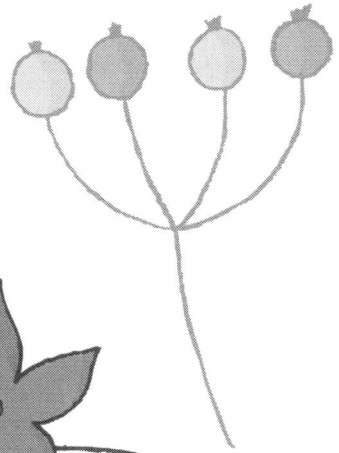

Thank You, Lord For...

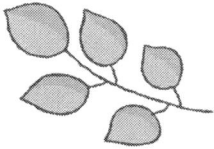

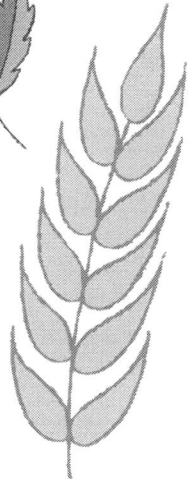

Date: _____

My Requests:

Bible Verse:

My Prayer:

Answers:

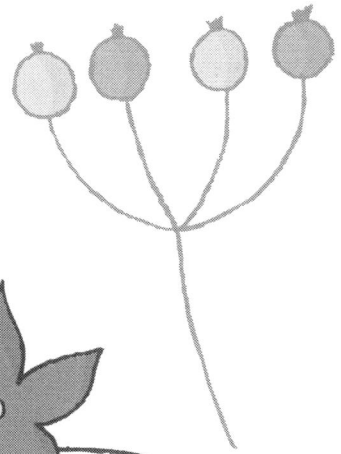

Thank You, Lord For...

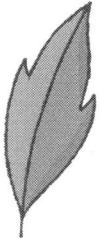

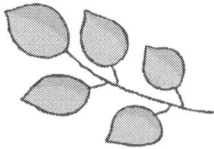

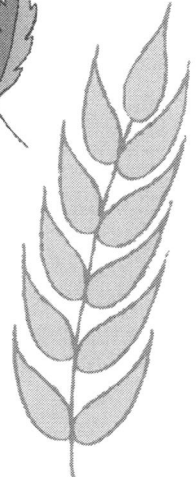

Date: _____

My Requests:

Bible Verse:

My Prayer:

Answers:

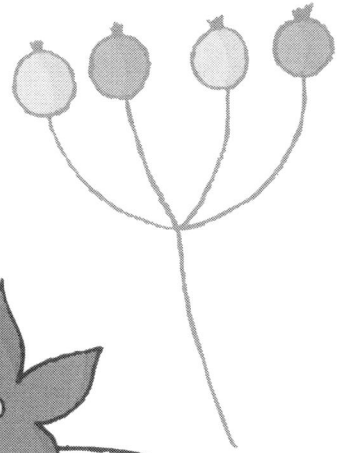

Thank You, Lord For...

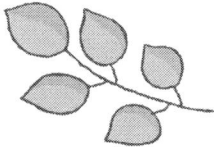

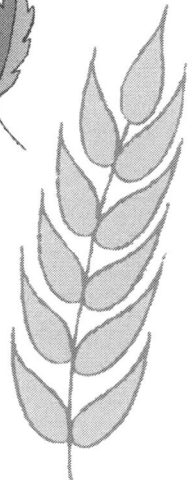

Date: _____

My Requests:

Bible Verse:

My Prayer:

Answers:

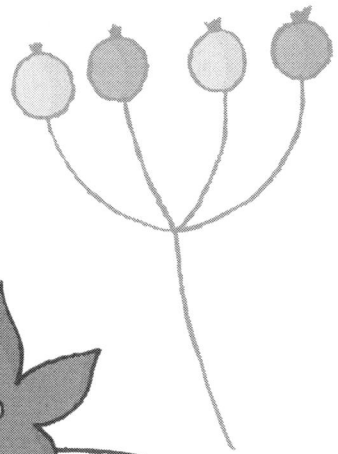

Thank You, Lord For...

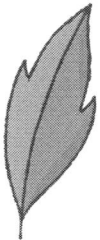

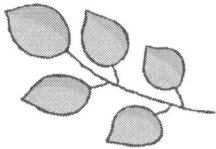

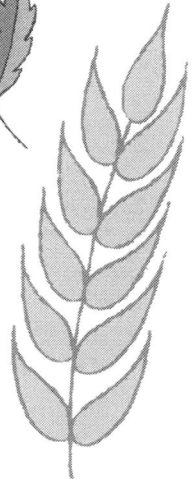

Date: _____

My Requests:

Bible Verse:

My Prayer:

Answers:

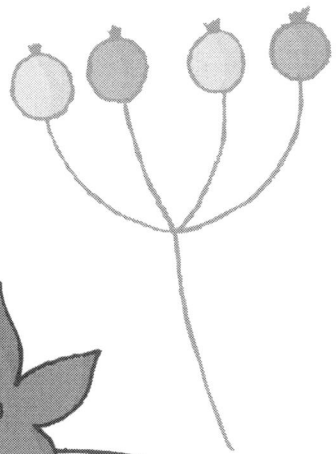

Thank You, Lord For...

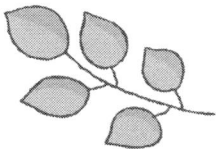

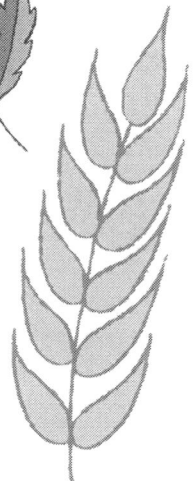

Date: _____

My Requests:

Bible Verse:

My Prayer:

Answers:

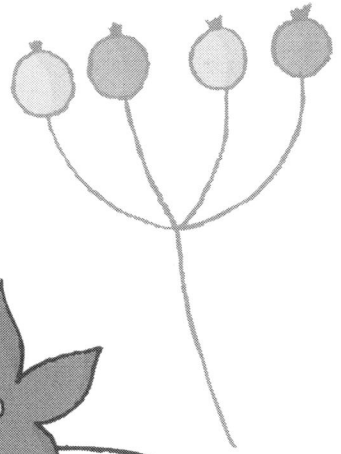

Thank You, Lord For...

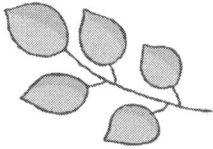

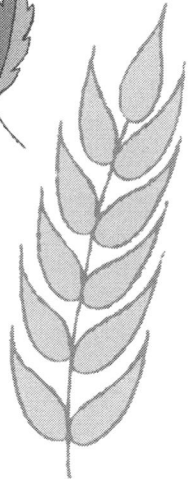

Date: _____

My Requests:

Bible Verse:

My Prayer:

Answers:

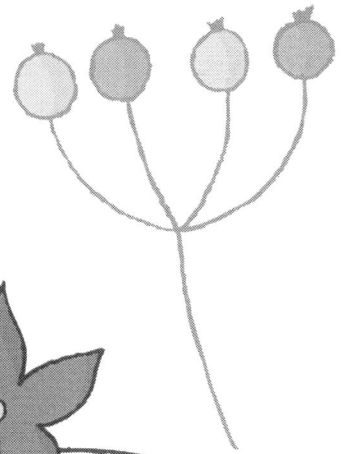

Thank You, Lord For...

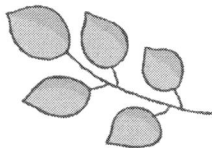

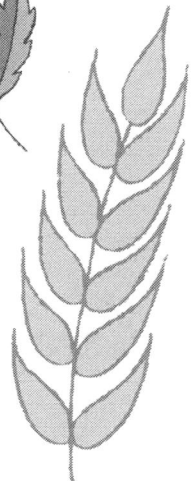

Date: _____

My Requests:

Bible Verse:

My Prayer:

Answers:

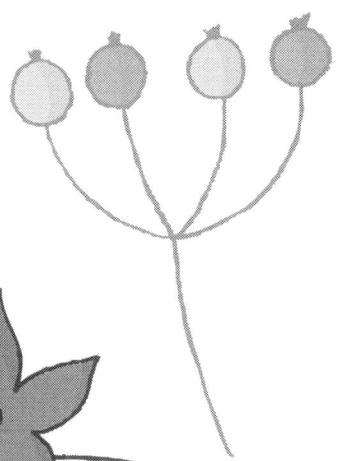

Thank You, Lord For...

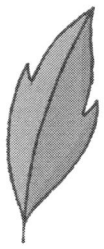

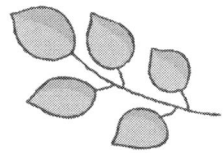

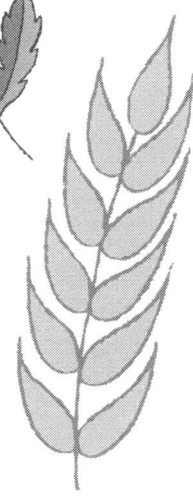

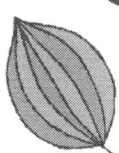

21108546R00075

EASY VEGAN

COOKBOOK

for beginners

Healthy and Delicious Recipes for VEGAN Diet Lovers
Start Eating Vegan Quickly and Easily

Erin Starless

Table of Contents

Introduction

Vegan diet yes or vegan diet no?

First of all, let's start by saying that when we talk about diet, we mean nutrition and not a reduced diet. So, let's start by debunking the myth that those who eat vegan do it to eat less. This is absolutely not true! Eating vegan is a lifestyle, a choice that respects the environment and your body. Being vegan does not mean giving something up. For example, there are many people who, due to their lifestyle, need to constantly improve their protein intake.

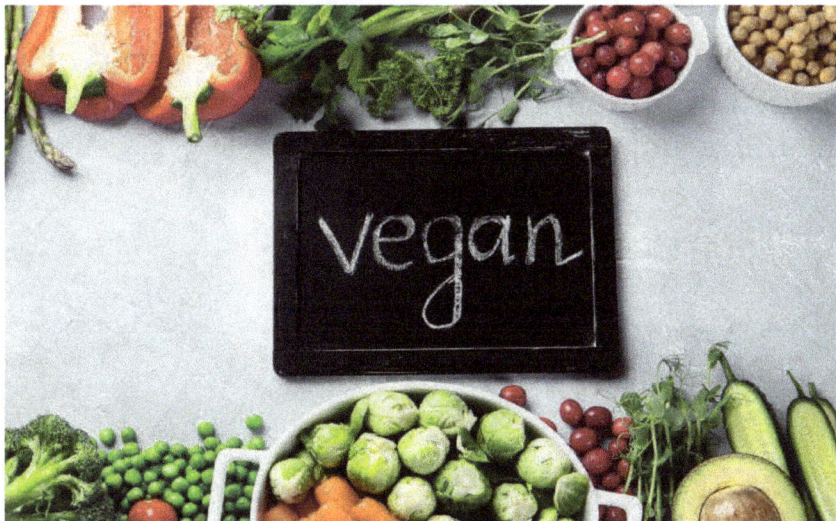

The common misconception is that a vegan diet cannot meet these needs because it is believed that a vegan diet, giving up animal-based foods, is low in protein.

Mental stamina is one of the most significant challenges people face when they decide to follow a vegan diet. In fact, while for a convinced vegan it is not difficult to follow their diet, for a person who approaches the vegan style for the first time it is much more complex. In fact, it is believed that the vegan diet involves many sacrifices from the point of view of taste or that it is generally too complex.

These common thoughts stem from the habit of always eating the same things and always in the same way. Even advertisements influence the common thought that in order to be able to satisfy the palate it is normal to have to eat only certain foods: a nice steak, a fast-food sandwich, fried bacon. Without foods of animal origin, it seems to be impossible to survive!

The purpose of this book is therefore to present a series of recipes that are not only rich in protein but also tasty and easy to prepare. In fact, approaching the vegan

What is a Vegan Diet?

Many people practice a vegan diet and many people talk about it, but there is still a lot of confusion about what a vegan diet actually entails. Sugars, carbohydrates, and fats, what they contain most of the time is not clear to most of us. There is too much confusion and a mistaken belief that there cannot be a vegan diet that can be nutritionally complete.

Instead, it is exactly the opposite. The vegan diet is perfect! In fact, a plant-based diet is rich in carbohydrates, abundant in protein, low in fat and rich in nutrients, minerals and antioxidants. All of this increases strength and endurance, improves aerobic capacity, reduces body fat and muscle fatigue. It is no coincidence that many athletes are using a vegan diet in order to improve their physical performance.

But... what foods to eat? We have to be honest: there's another common misconception among many people, even in the health and fitness industry: that anyone who switches to a vegan diet will automatically become super healthy. This is also not true. There are plenty of junk vegan foods out there, like frozen veggie pizza and dairy-free ice cream, that can really be counterproductive if eaten all the time. Engaging in healthy foods is the only way to get health benefits.

We must also pay attention to how certain products arrive in our pantry. Let's start by saying that whole foods are unprocessed foods that come from the earth. Today we eat some minimally processed foods such as fresh rice, whole wheat pasta, tofu, nuts, and seed butter. This is all fine as long as the processing is minimal.

Here are the different categories that define a vegan diet:

- o Legumes (basically lentils and beans) and whole grains.
- o Fruits and vegetables
- o Nuts and seeds (including nut butter)
- o Herbs and spices

All of the above categories make up an entire vegan diet.

How to prepare them is where it's fun, as is seasoning and cooking them, mixing and matching them to give them great taste and versatility in meals.

What to have in your pantry

Certainly, for those new to a vegan diet, the first step is to figure out what to put in the pantry. After all, it's not hard to imagine how big a difference there is from the previous classic diet.

You don't want to start making a recipe only to realize you're missing ingredients?

So, here's what to always have in the kitchen:

- **Non-Starchy Vegetables:** leafy greens (kale, spinach, butter lettuce, etc.), broccoli, zucchini, eggplant, tomatoes.
- **Starchy Vegetables:** all kinds of potatoes, whole corn, legumes (all beans and lentils), root vegetables, quinoa.
- **Fruits:** all whole fruits (avoid dried and juiced fruits).
- **Whole Grains:** 100% whole wheat, brown rice, and oats.
- **Beverages:** water, green tea, unsweetened vegan milk, decaffeinated coffee and tea.
- **Spices:** all spices.
- **Omega 3 Sources:** ground flax seed, chia seeds.
- **Nuts:** peanuts, almonds, cashews, walnuts.

You can also purchase the following foods, but remember to consume them sparingly:

Avocadoes - Coconuts - Sesame seeds - Sunflower seeds - Pumpkin seeds - Dried fruit - Added sweeteners (maple syrup, fruit juice concentrate, and natural sugars) - Caffeinated tea and coffee - Alcoholic beverages - Refined soy protein and wheat protein.

SNACKS

1. *Spicy Kale Chips*

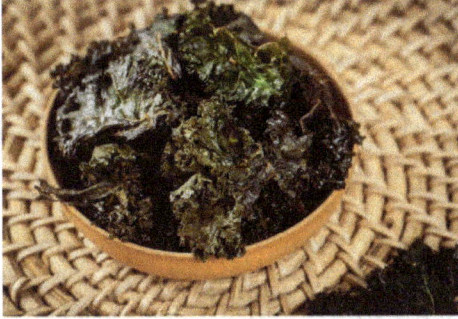

Course: Snacks

Prep Time: 15 minutes

Cook Time: 50 minutes

Total Time: 65 minutes

Servings: 2

Ingredients

- Kale (10 Oz.)
- Garlic Powder (.50 T.)
- Brown Sugar (.50 T.)
- Ancho (2 t.)
- Smoked Paprika (1 T.)
- Chili Powder (.10 t.)
- Nutritional Yeast (.25 C.)
- Minced Garlic (.50 t.)
- Salt (.25 t.)
- Ground Pepper (.50 t.)
- Sriracha (.50 t.)
- Lime Juice (1)
- Garlic Powder (1 t.)
- Sriracha (2 t.)

- Olive Oil (3 T.)

Directions:

- To make these delicious chips, you will first want to heat your oven to 275 degrees.
- Next, prepare your kale by removing the stems from the leaves. Once this is done, carefully tear the kale into pieces and then wash them. Carefully dry each piece of kale and place in a large bowl.
- In a separate bowl, you will want to combine the lime juice, zest from the lime, garlic powder, Sriracha, olive oil, pepper, and salt. Give everything a good stir to assure they are mixed together properly, and all of the flavors have a chance to blend together. Once this step is complete, pour the sauce over the kale and toss to coat.
- Now, you will want to line a baking sheet with some parchment paper. Once in place, carefully divide the kale in a single layer. When the kale is in place, bake in the oven for thirty-five to forty minutes. Halfway through this time, you will want to rotate your pan to assure even cooking.
- Finally, remove the pan from the oven, allow to cool, and enjoy your healthy chips!
-

2. Chocolate Almond Protein Bars

Course: Snacks

Prep Time: 20 minutes

Servings: 12 bars

Ingredients

- 170 grams raw almonds
- ¼ teaspoon of sea salt
- 1 teaspoon of cinnamon
- 150 grams rolled oats
- 140 grams plant-based vanilla protein powder
- 110 ml maple syrup
- 45 grams dairy-free chocolate chips (optional)

Preparation

- Using parchment paper or cooking spray to clean an eight-by-eight-inch square dish.
- Measure 42 grams of almonds, cut them and put them on top.
- Pour the remaining 126 grams of almonds and salt into a food processor. Heat until you have butter with almond, just a few minutes.

17

- Add oats, protein powder, cinnamon and maple syrup and continue processing until smooth.
- Use the back of a spoon to press the mixture into the pan. Top with the chopped almonds and press them into the bars.
- In a small glass cup, put the chocolate chips and microwave until melted. Drizzle the chocolate over the bars and allow for 20 minutes before cutting to be set in the refrigerator.
- Place unfilled bars in the fridge in an airtight container.

3. Candied Peanuts

Course: Snacks

Prep Time: 5 minutes

Cook Time: 10 minutes

Total Time: 15 minutes

Ingredients

- 2 cups peanuts, roasted & unsalted
- 1 tsp. lemon juice
- 1 cup sugar

Directions

- Over medium heat in a saucepan, melt the sugar completely, stirring frequently.
- Add lemon juice to the sugar only when the sugar reaches the consistency of corn syrup, stirring quickly.
- Remove the mixture from the heat & stir in the peanuts quickly. To make the coated peanuts hard, spread them on an oiled baking sheet.

Peanuts deserve an honorable mention: they contain 24 grams of protein per 100 grams and 16 grams of carbohydrates. This is a very interesting snack for all those who do a lot of sports and need continuous supply of protein.

4. Peanut Butter Power Bites

Course: Snacks

Prep Time: 5 minutes

Cook Time: 10 minutes

Total Time: 15 minutes

Servings: 4

Ingredients

- Peanut Butter (2 C.)
- Ground Almonds (.33 C.)
- Dehydrated Cranberries (.66 C.)
- Chia Seeds (.10 C.)
- Flax Seeds (.33 C.)
- Rolled Oats (2 C.)
- Grated Carrots (1.50 C.)
- Raw Honey (.50 C.)
- Vanilla Extract (1 t.)

Directions:

- To start, you are going to take all of the dry ingredients from the list above and mix them in a small mixing bowl. The last ingredient you will want to add in the grated carrots. Once in place, you can use a wooden spoon or your hands to combine everything.

- Next, you will slowly want to add in the vanilla extract, honey, and the peanut butter. As you mix everything together, you will notice your dough beginning to form. When you feel everything is combined well, pop the bowl into the fridge for about twenty minutes.
- Once this time has passed, you can remove the bowl and begin rolling bite-sized pieces of your dough. These snacks can be stored in the fridge or frozen if you plan on keeping them for a while!

5. *Cauliflower Popcorn*

Course: Snacks

Prep Time: 10 minutes

Cook Time: 60 minutes

Total Time: 70 minutes

Servings: 4

Ingredients

- 1 head cauliflower
- 4 tbsp. olive oil
- 1 tsp. salt, to taste

Directions

- Preheat your oven at 425 F/220 C.
- Trim the head of the cauliflower and discard the thick stems and core; cut the florets and make Ping-Pong balls size pieces.
- Mix the salt and olive oil together in a large bowl, whisk and then put the cauliflower pieces & toss thoroughly.

23

- For easy cleanup, line a baking sheet with parchment then spread the cauliflower pieces on the sheet & roast until most of the pieces have turned golden brown, approximately an hour, turning 4 or 5 times.

BREAKFAST

6. *Vegan-Edge Waffles*

Course: Breakfast

Prep Time: 15 minutes

Cook Time: 2 hours

Total Time: 135 minutes

Servings: 12 waffles

Ingredients:

- ¾ cup (180 ml) almond milk
- ¼ cup (55 g) packed dark brown or raw sugar
- One ¼-ounce (7 g) packet active dry yeast
- One 13.5-ounce (400 ml) can full-fat coconut milk
- 1½ teaspoons vanilla extract
- 4 cups (480 g) whole wheat pastry flour
- 1 teaspoon salt ½ cup (110 g) raw sugar cubes, crushed roughly into quarters with a mortar and pestle
- Oil, for greasing

Preparation

- Heat the almond milk in a small saucepan over medium heat until it is cooler than the temperature of your body. In the brown sugar and yeast, transfer to a large bowl and whisk. Set 5 minutes free.

27

- Scrape the solids in a small bowl from the coconut milk. Pour the liquid and comb until smooth. Drop the coffee. Fold the cream of coconut into the solution of almond milk.
- Whisk the flour and salt in 2 cups (240 g). Add another 180 g (1½ cups) of flour and turn to a wooden spoon when the dough begins to come together. It's going to be messy. Cover and set up for an hour in a hot, humid position to grow.
- Add the remaining ½ cup (60 g) of flour and the sugar cubes. The dough is going to be a bit sticky but still workable. (You should cool the dough overnight at this point.)
- Preheat the Belgian waffle iron and grease it. Break the dough into 12 balls equally. Place a ball of dough on the iron and tightly shut it. Cook until golden brown for about 6 minutes.
- Continue with the leftover dough and serve. (These waffles are thick, so break open your first one to see if it's fully cooked, because waffle iron varies. (Waffles can be individually wrapped in parchment paper and stored in an airtight container for up to 3 days or frozen for up to 3 months. To bake, toast in a 300 ° F/150 ° C oven until moist and crispy outside.)

7. *Sweet Potato and Orange Bread*

Course: Breakfast

Prep Time: 5 minutes

Cook Time: 50 minutes

Total Time: 55 minutes

Servings: 6

Ingredients

- 1 large sweet potato (about 12 oz.), peeled and shredded
- 1/2 cup fresh orange juice
- 1/3 cup water
- 1/3 cup orange marmalade
- 4 Tbsp canola oil
- 1 Tbsp arrowroot powder
- 3 cups flour self-rising
- 1/2 cup sugar
- 2 tsp baking powder
- 1/4 tsp salt

Directions:

- Preheat oven to 375 F/180 C.
- In a small saucepan, cook the shredded sweet potato for 10 min; drain and cool.

- In a bowl, combine shredder potato with orange juice, water, orange marmalade, canola oil, and arrowroot powder.
- In a separate bowl, combine together the flour, sugar, baking powder, and salt.
- Add the liquid ingredients to the flour mixture and stir just until combined.
- Spoon batter into greased loaf pan and bake for 30-35 minutes.
- When ready, allow it to cool for 10 minutes.
- Slice and serve.

8. Sweet French Toast

Course: Breakfast

Prep Time: 5 minutes

Cook Time: 10 minutes

Total Time: 15 minutes

Servings: 2

Ingredients

- 3 Tbsp olive oil
- 1 cup of soy milk (unsweetened)
- 1 cup oat flour (or buckwheat)
- 1/2 tsp cinnamon
- 2 Tbsp brown sugar or sugar
- 6 slices day-old bread (or multi-grain bread)

Servings

- vegan spread, groundnuts, honey or Maple syrup

Directions:

- Heat oil in a frying skillet over medium-high heat.
- Pour soy milk in one bowl.
- In a separate bowl, combine together oat flakes and brown sugar; stir well.
- Dip each bread slice first in soy milk, and then roll into oat flakes mixture.
- Fry your vegan French toast for a couple of minutes on each side, or until golden brown.
- Remove French toast onto a lined plate with kitchen paper to drain.
- Serve with your favorite vegan spread, groundnuts, honey or Maple syrup.

9. The Power of Banana & Soya Smoothie

Course: Breakfast

Prep Time: 5 minutes

Servings: 2

Ingredients

- 3/4 cup soya milk
- 2 bananas frozen
- 1 kiwi fruit sliced
- 1 Tbsp hemp seeds
- 1 Tbsp linseed oil
- 1 scoop vegan protein powder (pea or soy protein)
- 1 cup fresh spinach
- 3/4 cup frozen berries thawed (unsweetened)

Directions:

- Place all ingredients in your blender.
- Blend for about 45 seconds or until everything is well mixed.
- Serve.

10.   *Parsley and Almond Bread*

Course: Breakfast

Prep Time: 10 minutes

Cook Time: 1 hour

Servings: 2

Ingredients

- 1 1/2 cups sparkling water on room temperature
- 1 Tbsp of active dry yeast
- 1 tsp sugar
- 3 Tbsp olive oil
- 2 1/2 cups self-rising flour
- 2 Tbsp fresh minced parsley
- 1/2 cup almonds finely chopped
- 1 tsp ground garlic
- 1 tsp salt

Directions:

- Preheat oven to 375 F/185 C.
- Grease a baking loaf with olive oil; set aside.

- In a large bowl, dissolve yeast, sugar, and salt in sparkling water; let stand until bubbles form on the surface.
- Add in flour and olive oil and beat until smooth.
- Add all remaining ingredients, and continue to beat until combined well or until form soft dough.
- Turn onto a floured surface; knead until smooth and elastic or for about 8 minutes.
- Shape dough into a loaf, and place into a prepared bread loaf.
- Bake for 30 to 35 minutes or until golden brown.
- Remove from oven, and let sit for 10 minutes.
- Slice and serve.

11.   *Sour Edamame Spread*

Course: Breakfast

Prep Time: 5 minutes

Cook Time: 5 minutes

Total Time: 10 minutes

Servings: 6

Ingredients

- 2 cups frozen unshelled edamame, cooked according to package directions
- 1/4 cup sesame oil
- 1 cup silken tofu, drained
- 1 Tbsp minced garlic (from 3 medium cloves)
- Flaky sea salt to taste
- White pepper to taste
- 2 tsp ground cumin
- 1 Tbsp rice vinegar
- 4 Tbsp fresh lemon juice
- Sesame seeds for serving

Directions:

- Place all ingredients into your high-speed blender or into a food processor.

- Blend until combined well.
- Transfer spread to a bowl and a sprinkle with sesame seeds.
- Edamame spread can be refrigerated in an airtight container up to 3 days.

The spread is creamy, low-fat and ideal to serve with some crunchy rice crackers or cucumber slices.

12.   *Tofu Omelette*

Course: Breakfast

Prep Time: 8 minutes

Cook Time: 12 minutes

Total Time: 20 minutes

Servings: 2

Ingredients

- 2 Tbsp of olive oil
- 1 small onion finely chopped
- 1 large red pepper chopped
- 1/2 cup white mushrooms halved or sliced
- 3/4 lb tofu cut into cubes
- 1 Tbsp nutritional yeast
- 1 tsp turmeric (for color)
- 1 tsp of garlic powder
- Sea salt and ground black pepper to taste

Directions:

- Heat oil in a large frying pan over medium-high heat.
- Sauté onion and red pepper with a pinch of salt for 2 to 3 minutes.

- Add mushrooms and cook until most of the water from the mushrooms has evaporated.
- Add tofu cubes and all remaining ingredients; stir well.
- Cover and cook over medium heat for about 6 to 8 minutes; stir occasionally.
- Taste and adjust seasonings.
- Serve hot.

13.   *Pumpkin Spice Latte*

Course: Breakfast

Prep Time: 10 minutes

Ingredients

- 1 shot espresso or brewed coffee
- ½ cup almond milk
- 2 tablespoons pumpkin puree
- 1 tablespoon full-fat coconut milk
- 2 tablespoons heavy whipping cream
- Cinnamon, to taste
- Pinch of nutmeg, to taste
- Cloves, to taste
- Cardamom, to taste
- Ginger, to taste
- Stevia or low-carb sweetener of choice
- 1 teaspoon vanilla extract

Optional

- 1 teaspoon MCT Oil or Ghee Butter

Preparation

- Heat a sauce pan over low heat.
- Add the pumpkin puree and the spices – cinnamon, nutmeg, cloves, ginger, cardamom, and stir well.
- Stir constantly for 2 to 3 minutes, until mixture is fragrant.
- Add the milk and continue stirring. Cook until warm, but not boiling! When the mixture is warm, add in the stevia and the vanilla extract.
- Pour your coffee into a mug.
- Then pour the pumpkin-milk mixture over the coffee and top with heavy whipped cream.
- Sprinkle with cinnamon, if you wish.
- If you want, you can add the MCT oil to the coffee before adding the pumpkin-latte. Warm your soul with this delicious beverage!

14.   *Dragon Fruit Smoothie*

Course: Breakfast

Prep Time: 5 minutes

Cook Time: 10 minutes

Total Time: 15 minutes

Ingredients

- 1 Dragon fruit (red) about 3/4 lb
- 1 large ripe banana
- 1 cup of coconut milk
- 1/2 cup of shredded coconut
- 3 Tbsp ground nuts
- 1 cup of baby spinach fresh
- 1 scoop vegan protein powder (soy or pea)

- 1 glass of crushed ice cubes

Directions:

- Cut the dragon fruit in half.
- With the help of a sharp knife slice right through it, scoop out the flesh with a spoon.

43

- Place dragon fruit flesh in your blender along with all remaining ingredients.
- Blend it until completely smooth.

This Dragon Fruit Smoothie is an exciting way to incorporate more fruit into your diet.

15.   *Carrots and Raisins Muffin*

Course: Breakfast

Prep Time: 5 minutes

Cook Time: 30 minutes

Total Time: 35 minutes

Servings: 4

Ingredients

- 1 1/4 cup almond flour
- 1/2 cup whole grain flour (any)
- 3 Tbsp ground almonds
- 2 cups carrot, grated
- 1 1/2 tsp baking soda
- 2 tsp baking powder
- 2 tsp cinnamon
- 1/2 tsp salt
- 1 tsp apple vinegar
- 1/2 cup extra-virgin olive oil
- 2 Tbsp linseed oil
- 4 Tbsp organic honey
- 3 oz raisins seedless

Directions:

- Preheat oven to 360 F.
- In a big bowl, combine together almond flour, whole grain flour, baking soda, baking powder, cinnamon, and salt.
- In a separate bowl, whisk apple vinegar, olive oil, linseed oil, and honey.
- Combine almond flour mixture with liquid mixture; stir well.
- Add in the shredded carrots and raisins; stir well.
- Fill the muffin cups 3/4 of the way full.
- Bake for 30 minutes.
- Remove from the oven, and allow to cool for 10 minutes.
- Serve.

16.   *Green Tornado Smoothie*

Course: Breakfast

Prep Time: 5 minutes

Cook Time: 5 minutes

Total Time: 10 minutes

Servings: 2

Ingredients

- 1 avocado (diced)
- 1 cup fresh spinach (chopped)
- 1 cup fresh peppermint leaves, chopped
- 1 banana frozen or fresh
- 1 cup coconut milk canned
- 1/2 cup shredded coconut
- 1/2 cup ground nuts (almonds, peanuts)
- 1 scoop vegan pea protein powder
- 2 Tbsp extracted honey (or to taste)
- Ice cubes

Directions:

- Place all ingredients in your high-speed blender and blend until smooth.
- Serve in chilled glasses with ice cubes.

17.   *Nutty Silken Tofu with Berries Smoothie*

Course: Breakfast

Prep Time: 5 minutes

Cook Time: 5 minutes

Total Time: 10 minutes

Servings: 2

Ingredients

- 1 cup of soy milk
- 1/2 cup of silken tofu
- 1 Tbsp almond butter (unsweetened)
- 1 frozen banana sliced
- 2 Tbsp Steel-cut oatmeal
- 2 Tbsp ground almonds
- 2 Tbsp ground cashews
- 1 tsp pure vanilla extract
- 1 cup fresh or frozen berries (blueberries, raspberries, blackberries, and strawberries)
- 2 Tbsp agave or maple syrup

Directions:

- Add all ingredients in your high-speed blender.
- Blend until smooth.
- Serve and enjoy your liquid breakfast.

18.   *Breakfast Sandwich*

Course: Breakfast

Prep Time: 10 minutes

Cook Time: 10 minutes

Total Time: 20 minutes

Servings: 3

Ingredients

- 1 tablespoon of coconut oil (or preferred cooking oil)
- 1 14 oz container extra firm tofu, pressed & cut lengthwise into 6 even slices
- 1 teaspoon of turmeric
- ½ teaspoon of garlic powder
- ½ teaspoon of Kala Namak (black salt) (sub regular salt)
- 3 melty vegan cheese slices
- 6 slices of bread, 3 or wraps (gluten-free if preferred)
- 1-2 tablespoons vegan mayo
- 1 cup of greens (spinach, spring mix, green lettuce, romaine, etc.)
- 1-2 medium tomatoes, sliced thin
- 6 pickle slices
- Fresh cracked pepper, to taste

Preparation

- Season the salt, garlic powder, cracked pepper, and turmeric on one side of the tofu. When it's time to flip them, you'll season the second side in the pan.
- Heat oil over medium heat in a medium pan and put the slices of seasoned tofu side down on the pan. While cooking is on the bottom side, season the

top side. Let the tofu cook until mildly brown and crispy for 3 to 5 minutes. Then flip the slices and cook for 3-5 minutes on the other side. Now is a good time, if desired, to put bread in a toaster.

- Put 2 slices of tofu side by side on a baking sheet with a slice of cheese on top of each package to melt the cheese. Place it 1-3 minutes in the oven on broil until the cheese is melted. A toaster oven can also be used.
- Spread mayo on the bread on both ends. Put on one hand the 2 slices of tofu with cheese. Sprinkle with salt and pepper if desired, add the greens and tomatoes. Then add a few pickle slices and bring together the sandwich. Slice diagonally.

Start your morning off right with this Vegan Breakfast Sandwich. It's hearty, savory & oh-so satisfying!

LUNCH/DINNER

19. *Basil Pesto*

Course: Lunch/Dinner

Prep Time: 10 minutes

Ingredients

- 2 cups Fresh Basil Pressed into measuring cup
- 4 Garlic Cloves
- 1/3 cup pine nuts
- 2/3 cup grated vegan parmesan cheese
- 1/2 cup olive oil
- 1 teaspoon of Salt
- 1 teaspoon of Pepper

Ingredients for Parmesan Cheese

- ¾ cup raw cashews
- 3 tbsp of nutritional yeast
- ¾ tsp sea salt
- ¼ tsp garlic powder

Preparation for Vegan Parmesan Cheese

Add all the four ingredients into a food processor and mix/pulse until a fine meal is achieved. Parmesan cheese that you will not use for the recipe can be stored in the refrigerator.

Preparation

- Put the basil, garlic, pine nuts, and parmesan cheese into a food processor. Pulse until chunky. Add the Olive oil in slowly whilst the food processor is still on until it has all been added.
- Add the salt and pepper. Enjoy!

20.   *Chickpea, Tofu, and Eggplant Curry*

Course: Lunch/Dinner

Prep Time: 5 minutes

Cook Time: 30 minutes

Total Time: 35 minutes

Servings: 4

Ingredients

- 2 tablespoons coconut oil, divided
- 1 package of medium-firm tofu, cubed and dried with paper towel
- 3 long Asian eggplants, quartered into 3-inch strips
- ½ large onion, very thinly sliced (use a mandolin, if you have one)
- 2 tablespoons minced ginger
- 4 garlic cloves, minced
- 1 tablespoon garam masala
- ½ tablespoon each: cumin seeds, turmeric, sea salt
- Optional: ½ – 1 teaspoon chili flakes
- ¼ cup tomato paste
- 1 can coconut milk
- ½ can water
- 1 15-ounce can chickpeas, drained and rinsed
- Cilantro, to serve

Preparation

- In a big, non-stick frying pan, heat ½ tablespoon of coconut oil over medium to high heat. Remove the tofu and fried for about 5 minutes until golden brown on 2 sides. Clear from the breadboard.
- In the tofu bowl, steam 1 tablespoon of coconut oil. Brown the eggplant on all hands, if possible, operating in lots. Remove from the pan the eggplant.
- Heat the remaining ½ tablespoon of coconut oil in an eggplant pan. Add the onion and cook 2-3 minutes or until smooth. Add the garlic and ginger and cook for 1 minute. Attach the garam masala, cumin seeds and turmeric to the pan and make toast for 1 minute, continuously stirring. Stirring constantly, add the sea salt, optional chili flakes (if used) and tomato paste and simmer for 1 minute.
- Apply the coconut milk and water to the saucepan, bring to a boil and stir and scrape the bottom for any pieces. Return the eggplant to the pan and turn the heat down. Let the eggplant cook for 12-15 minutes, uncovered, or until tender but not mushy.
- In the curry, mix the chickpeas and tofu and let them heat up. Serve on top with some rice (or cauliflower rice, my favorite) and some cilantro.

21.   *Lentil Spinach Soup*

Course: Lunch/Dinner

Prep Time: 15 minutes

Cook Time: 30 minutes

Total Time: 45 minutes

Servings: 4

Ingredients

- 1 onion
- 1-2 carrots
- 3 cloves garlic
- 1 cup green/brown lentils (uncooked)
- 15 oz. can of tomato (diced)
- 4 cups vegetable broth
- 3 oz. spinach
- 1 tsp. cumin
- ½ tablespoon of smoked paprika
- ¼ tablespoon of salt (more to taste)

Preparation

- Dice both the onion and carrot.
- Saute onion and carrot in a stockpot over medium - high heat for about 7 minutes.

- Meanwhile, thin garlic and rinse lentils. (use 3 Tbsp. water / broth for oil-free saute method.)
- Apply to the stockpot garlic, cumin, smoked paprika and salt. Saute for one minute.
- Add lentils, tomatoes and broth. Heat up and bring to a boil.
- Add water, cover and cook for approximately 30 minutes or until lentils are tender.
- In the meantime, cut the spinach finely.
- In the last few minutes of cooking, add spinach.
- Taste the salt. (Or before eating, add a hot sauce dash!)

22.   *Quinoa Stuffed Poblano Peppers*

Course: Lunch/Dinner

Prep Time: 10 minutes

Cook Time: 45 minutes

Total Time: 55 minutes

Servings: 4

Ingredients

- 4 poblano peppers
- 2 teaspoons olive oil, divided, plus more for the peppers
- 3/4 cup red quinoa
- 1 cup low sodium vegetable broth
- 1 medium yellow onion, chopped
- 1 garlic clove, chopped
- ½ cup cooked corn, thawed if frozen
- 1 cup low sodium canned black beans, rinsed and drained
- 1 4 ounce can mild diced green chiles
- 1 teaspoon chili powder
- 1/2 teaspoon ground cumin
- Coarse kosher salt and freshly ground black pepper
- 3 tablespoons unsoaked nuts (or diced tofu for a very soft texture)
- Chopped fresh cilantro, optional
- Vegan yogurt no fat, optional

Preparation

- Preheat the broiler to the top and place the rack of the oven in the second place.
- Rub olive oil poblanos and put a healthy baking dish in a well-seasoned cast iron skillet or oiled oven. Broil until the pepper's skin is blistered, 5-10 minutes per side beginning to shine. Take from the oven the peppers and place them in a pan. Tightly cover the top with plastic wrap and allow 5-10 minutes to rest. Move the rack of the oven down to the center position and heat the oven to 375 F.
- Put quinoa in a fine mesh strainer while the peppers are broiling and rinse under cold water for 2 minutes. Heat 1 teaspoon of olive oil over medium heat in a medium-sized pot. When dry, add the quinoa and toast for 1 minute, stirring. Add the broth of vegetables and ½ cup water. Bring to a boil, cover, and lower to moderate low heat. Allow the quinoa to cook uninterrupted, about 15 minutes until all the liquid is absorbed. Remove from the heat and allow another 5 minutes for the quinoa to sit, covered.
- In the meantime, melt 1 tablespoon of olive oil over medium heat in a shallow skillet. Once hot, add the garlic and onions. Cook, frequently stirring, for 5-7 minutes, before softened and just starting to brown.
- Mix quinoa, onions, garlic, peas, beans, green chilies, cumin, salt and pepper to taste in a large bowl.
- Remove the peppers and remove the skins from the bowl. They should easily peel off, but don't worry about getting off every last bit. Cut each pepper carefully in half and remove the seeds. In the same dish, you broiled them in, arrange peppers cut side up. Fill them with the mixture of quinoa evenly and sprinkle with the unsoaked nuts (or diced tofu).
- Cook the stuffed peppers in the oven for about 15 minutes until cooked through. If needed, sprinkle with chopped cilantro and vegan yogurt.

23. *Harissa Baked Tofu*

Course: Lunch/Dinner

Prep Time: 20 minutes

Cook Time: 30 minutes

Total Time: 50 minutes

Servings: 3

Ingredients

- 1 tablespoon olive oil (OF: ¼ cup/60 ml broth)
- 1 yellow onion, chopped fine
- 1 red or yellow bell pepper, chopped fine
- 3 garlic cloves, minced
- 1 tablespoon Harissa
- ¼ teaspoon ground turmeric
- 2 tablespoons tomato paste
- One 28-ounce (794 g) can diced tomatoes with juice
- 1 cup (240 ml) water ¼ teaspoon salt
- Two 16-ounce (454 g) packages sprouted or extra-firm tofu, drained and sliced into 12 pieces

Preparation

- Preheat the oven to a temperature of 200 ° C.
- Place a large, thick, medium-heat oven-proof skillet. To brush the pan, add the oil and stir, then add the onion. Cook, stirring frequently, about 5 minutes until the onion starts to soften. Add the garlic and bell peppers and cook for 3 minutes. Attach the harissa and curcuma and simmer for about 2 minutes until fragrant.
- Remove the tomato paste and cook until dark for 1 minute, stirring frequently. Add the tomatoes with their juice, water, and salt, nestle the tofu in the sauce, and heat up to medium-high. Remove from heat, cover, and switch to the oven once the tomatoes begin bubbling.
- Cook for 15 minutes, remove the lid and cook for a further 15 minutes until the tomato sauce is bubbly. Serve.

24.   *Vegan Chilli Sin Carne*

Course: Lunch/Dinner

Prep Time: 10 minutes

Cook Time: 30 minutes

Total Time: 40 minutes

Servings: 6

Ingredients

- 2 tablespoons of olive oil
- 3 cloves of garlic, minced
- 1 large red onion, thinly sliced
- 2 celery stalks, finely chopped
- 2 medium carrots, peeled and finely chopped
- 2 red peppers, roughly chopped
- 1 tablespoon of ground cumin
- 1 tablespoon of chili powder
- Salt and pepper, to taste
- 800 g tinned chopped tomatoes
- 400 g tin of red kidney beans, drained and rinsed
- 100 g split red lentils
- 400 g frozen soy mince
- 250 ml vegetable stock

Optional add-ins

- 1 tablespoon of miso paste
- 2 tablespoons of balsamic vinegar
- A large handful of fresh coriander, roughly chopped

To serve

- Cooked basmati rice
- Extra chopped coriander
- A squeeze of lime juice

Preparation

- In a large bowl, warm the olive oil.
- Stir the garlic, cabbage, celery, carrots, and peppers over moderate heat for a few minutes until tender.
- Stir and stir in cumin, chili powder, salt, and pepper.
- Mix in the chopped tomatoes, kidney beans, lentils, thin soy, and stock of vegetables. Add additional colors, if used.
- Leave for 25 minutes to cook.
- Serve with some basmati rice, fresh torn coriander, and lime juice squeeze.

Great freezes. Keeps refrigerated for up to four days.

25.   *Chickpea, Mango and Curried Cauliflower Salad*

Course: Lunch/Dinner

Prep Time: 10 minutes

Cook Time: 25 minutes

Total Time: 35 minutes

Servings: 4

Ingredients

- 1 teaspoon curry powder
- 1 teaspoon sugar
- 1 teaspoon ground mustard
- 1 teaspoon ground coriander
- ½ teaspoon ground turmeric
- ½ teaspoon ground cumin
- 3 tablespoons olive oil more as needed
- 1 medium yellow onion thinly sliced
- 1 cup canned chickpeas drained, rinsed and warmed through slightly
- 1 head of cauliflower cut into 1-inch florets, blanch for 2 minutes in boiling water and then pat dry
- 2 large mangoes peeled, pitted and chopped into ½-inch pieces
- 1 jalapeno stemmed, seeded and diced small
- 1 cup chopped cilantro
- 2 tablespoons lime juice
- 2 cups baby spinach
- 1 cup baby arugula
- Salt and black pepper

Preparation

- Blend the curry powder, cinnamon, ground mustard, coriander, cumin, ½ teaspoon of kosher salt, and ¼ teaspoon black pepper in a small bowl. Set it aside.
- Put the olive oil in a large skillet. Add the onion and cook at high heat for about 6 minutes. Attach the mixture of spices and turn the heat to medium-low. Cook an extra 6 minutes. Move to a wide bowl and add to the same bowl the chickpeas. Keep the pan at medium heat.
- Add the cauliflower to the same pan where the onion was cooked. If required, add more olive oil. Cook in the remaining spice mixture for about 5 minutes or until the cauliflower is seasoned and cooked clean. Use the onion and chickpeas to transfer the cauliflower to the bowl. Let sit for approximately 20 minutes at room temperature.
- Apply the pineapple, jalapeno, coriander, lime juice, spinach, and arugula to the dish. Toss in order to disperse the ingredients evenly. Adjust seasoning to taste and serve as soon as possible.

26.   *Chickpea and Mushroom Burger*

Course: Lunch/Dinner

Prep Time: 20 minutes

Cook Time: 15 minutes

Total Time: 35 minutes

Servings: 4

Ingredients

- 240g (9oz) chickpeas (about 1 tin drained weight)
- 2 level tablespoons gram flour (chickpea flour)
- 1 small red onion
- 2 large cloves garlic
- 75g tasty mushrooms (small handful)
- 1 tablespoon tahini
- Half teaspoon sea salt
- Half medium sized apple
- 1 teaspoon dried parsley
- 1 tablespoon fresh rosemary (finely chopped)
- 1 medium sized tomato

Preparation

- Crush the garlic, slice the cabbage, and cut the mushrooms into small pieces; saute for a few minutes in a saucepan.
- Coarsely mash chickpeas with a potato masher or fork in a large mixing bowl. It's a bit of work to get there, really! The mash doesn't have to be completely smooth, though you need to give it a thorough pressing

through so much of its pretty mushy. Leaving a few rustic-looking pieces is perfect.

- Cut the apple in half (including skin).
- Add the gram flour, tahini, salt, and apple and mix with the back of a metal spoon (to help press down and support the binding process).
- Split the rosemary into small pieces and cut the tomato.
- Place the sauteed things in the bowl together with all remaining ingredients, press down, and vigorously mix with a metal spoon.
- Divide into 4 and mold firmly into patties.
- Place on a grill tray and heat on each side for about 8 minutes (or until nicely tanned) under a medium grill.

27.   *Tempeh Vegetarian Chili*

Course: Lunch/Dinner

Prep Time: 5 minutes

Cook Time: 25 minutes

Total Time: 30 minutes

Servings: 4

Ingredients

- 2 tablespoons of olive oil 30 mL
- 1 8-oz package tempeh 226 g, roughly grated
- 1 medium white onion diced
- 1 red bell pepper diced
- 1 stalk celery diced
- 2 cloves garlic minced
- 3/4 cup tomato sauce 177 mL
- 1 15-oz can kidney beans 425 g, drained
- 1 15-oz can black beans 425 g, drained
- 1 cup water 240 mL
- 1 tablespoon of cumin and salteach
- ¼ tablespoon of each chili powder and crushed red pepper flakes
- To serve: chopped green onions, plain Greek yogurt

Preparation

- Brown Tempeh: warm the oil in a large pot over medium / high heat. Attach the tempeh and cook for about 5 minutes until lightly browned. It's all right if some of it sticks to the pan's bottom. Once you add the fluids, it'll come off.

- Add Flavor Makers: add onion, pepper bell, celery and garlic, cook until veggies are slightly soft, about 5 minutes.
- Prepare Everything: add the remaining ingredients, reduce heat to medium, and prepare for about 15 minutes until hot and mixed. Taste the seasonings and change them as needed. Complete and serve with green onions.

28.   *Vegan Tacos*

Course: Lunch/Dinner

Prep Time: 5 minutes

Cook Time: 10 minutes

Total Time: 15 minutes

Servings: 2

Ingredients:

- Taco Shells (8)
- Corn (.25 C.)
- Chopped Cherry Tomatoes (8)
- Chopped Avocado (1)
- Ground Cumin (2 t.)
- Hot Sauce (2 t.)
- Tomato Puree (1 C.)
- Black Beans (2 C.)

Directions:

- To begin this recipe, you will want to take a pan and place it over medium heat. As the pan begins to warm up, add in the tomato puree, black beans, hot sauce, and cumin. Cook all of these ingredients together for about five minutes or until everything is warmed through. At this point, feel free to season the dish however you would like.

- Next, you will begin to assemble the tacos. All you need to do is pour in as much or as little bean mixture into each taco

29.   *Spicy Kung Pao Tofu*

Course: Lunch/Dinner

Prep Time: 10 minutes

Cook Time: 35 minutes

Total Time: 45 minutes

Servings: 4

Ingredients:

- Water (1 T.)
- Sesame Oil (1 t.)
- Black Vinegar (2 t.)
- Cornstarch (1 t.)
- Sugar (2 t.)
- Dark Soy Sauce (2 t.)
- Light Soy Sauce (1 T.)
- Scallions (5)
- Sliced Root Ginger (1 In.)
- Minced Garlic (3)
- Sliced Red Pepper (1)
- Sliced Green Pepper (1)
- Cooking Oil (3 T.)
- Extra-firm Tofu (1 Lb.)

Directions:

- Much like with any tofu you cook, you are going to want to make sure you have pressed all of the liquid out. Please take the time to press your tofu before you begin cooking, this will leave you with the best results.

75

Once drained, you can cut your tofu into small cubes. At this point, you will also want to cut your green and red pepper into small pieces as well.

- Next, you will be making the sauce. You can do this by taking a small bowl and mix together the sugar, water, vinegar, cornstarch, garlic, green onion, ginger, salt, and both soy sauces. Be sure to mix everything together well to blend the flavors together.

- Next, you will want to take a skillet and place it over medium heat. As the pan warms up, add in three tablespoons of your oil and then gently place the tofu cubes. You will cook the tofu until it becomes a nice golden-brown color on all sides. Once your tofu is cooked, add in the peppers and cook them for another five minutes or so. By the end, the pepper will be nice and tender.

- Finally, you will gently pour in the sauce you made earlier. Be sure to stir the ingredients well, so the tofu becomes well coated. Cook this dish over medium heat for another five minutes or so to allow the sauce to begin to thicken.

30.   *Lentil Burgers*

Course: Lunch/Dinner

Prep Time: 5 minutes

Cook Time: 25 minutes

Total Time: 30 minutes

Servings: 4

Ingredients:

- Bread Crumbs (2 T.)
- Crushed Walnuts (2 T.)
- Soy Sauce (1 t.)
- Cooked Lentils (2 C.)
- Salt (.50 t.)
- Cumin (.25 t.)
- Nutritional Yeast (.25 C.)

Directions:

- First, you will want to cook your two cups of lentils. You will want to complete this task following the directions provided on the side of the package. Once this step is complete, drain the lentils and place them into a medium-sized bowl. When the lentils are in place, gently mash them until they reach a smooth consistency.
- At this point, you will want to add in the bread crumbs, crushed walnuts, soy sauce, nutritional yeast, cumin, and the salt. Be sure to

mix everything together and then begin to form your patties. They should be about four inches in diameter and only an inch thick.

- With your patties formed, you will want to heat a medium size pan over medium heat and begin to warm it. Once warm, add in oil and cook each patty for two to three minutes on each side. By the end, each side of the burger should be crisp and brown.

31. *Noodle Alfredo*

Course: Lunch/Dinner

Prep Time: 5 minutes

Cook Time: 25 minutes

Total Time: 30 minutes

Servings: 4

Ingredients:

- Green Peas (1 C.)
- Vegan Parmesan Cheese (.25 C.)
- Garlic Powder (.50 t.)
- Nutritional Yeast (6 T.)
- Pepper (.25 t.)
- Salt (.25 t.)
- Unsweetened Almond Milk (2 C.)
- All Purpose Flour (2 T.)
- Minced Garlic (4)
- Olive Oil (3 T.)
- Linguini (10 Oz.)
-

Directions:

- First things first—you will want to cook your linguini. Once this step is complete, drain the water and set the cooked pasta to the side for now.
- Next, you will take a large skillet and place it over medium heat. As the pan warms up, carefully add in your garlic and olive oil. You will want to stir these to assure nothing burns to the bottom of your pan.

- When you begin to smell the garlic, turn the heat down a tad. Once this is done, add in the flour and cook for about a minute in the olive oil alone. Next, you will add in the almond milk a little bit at a time. Be sure to whisk the ingredients together to help avoid forming clumps in your sauce. Go ahead and cook this sauce for another two minutes or so.
- Once your sauce is done, remove from the heat and allow it to cool for a minute or so. When it is safe to handle, transfer the liquid into a blender. When it is in place, add in the garlic, nutritional yeast, vegan parmesan cheese, pepper, and salt according to your taste. Go ahead and blend the mixture on high until you create a nice smooth and creamy sauce. Feel free to adjust your seasonings as you go.
- Next, you will want to return the sauce to your pan and place it over medium heat until it begins to bubble. Once the bubbles form, turn the heat to low and allow the sauce to thicken. Remember to stir your dish frequently to avoid it burning to the bottom.
- As you stir the sauce, add more milk if it is too thick. If the sauce is too thin, remove some liquid and add in some extra flour. When the sauce is ready, add it to your pasta and top with cooked peas.

32.   *Spinach and Red Lentil Masala*

Course: Dinner/Dinner

Prep Time: 5 minutes

Cook Time: 40minutes

Total Time: 45 minutes

Servings: 4

Ingredients:

- Baby Spinach (2 C.)
- Red Lentils (1 C.)
- Coconut Milk (15 Oz.)
- Salt (1 t.)
- Diced Tomatoes (15 Oz.)
- Coriander (.25 t.)
- Garam Masala (1 t.)
- Ground Cumin (1 t.)
- Chili Pepper (1)
- Minced Ginger (1 In.)
- Minced Garlic (2)
- Diced Red Onion (1)
- Olive Oil (1 T.)

Directions:

- To begin, place a large pot over a medium to high heat. As the pot warms up, you can add in your tablespoon of olive oil and the onion.

Cook the onion for five minutes or until it becomes soft. Once it does, you can add in the coriander, garam masala, cumin, chili pepper, ginger, and the garlic. When everything is in place, cook the ingredients for an extra two to three minutes.

- Once the ingredients from the step above are warmed through, you will want to carefully add the tomatoes and season everything with salt according to your taste. If there are any brown bits on the bottom of the pan, be sure to scrape them up and keep stirring everything. As you continue to cook, the liquid should reduce in about five minutes.

- Next, pour in the coconut milk along with one cup of water. Once in place, turn the heat up to high and bring the pot to a boil. At this point, you can add in the lentils and reduce the heat back to medium or so. Now, cook the lentils for twenty-five to thirty-five minutes. By the end, the lentils should be nice and tender!

- Finally, fold in your spinach and cook for an additional five minutes. Once the spinach has wilted, remove the pot from the heat and allow to cool slightly. You can serve this delicious meal over coconut rice or enjoy it by itself.

33. *Sweet Hawaiian Burger*

Course: Lunch/Dinner

Prep Time: 5 minutes

Cook Time: 40minutes

Total Time: 45 minutes

Servings: 4

Ingredients:

- Panko Breadcrumbs (1 C.)
- Red Kidney Beans (14 Oz.)
- Vegetable Oil (1 T.)
- Diced Sweet Potato (1.50 C.)
- Minced Garlic (1)
- Soy Sauce (2 T.)
- Apple Cider Vinegar (3 T.)
- Maple Syrup (.50 C.)
- Water (.50 C.)
- Tomato Paste (.50 C.)
- Pineapple Rings (4)
- Salt (.25 t.)
- Pepper (.25 t.)
- Cayenne (.10 t.)
- Ground Cumin (1.50 t.)
- Burger Buns (4)
- Optional: Red Onion, Tomato, Lettuce, Vegan Mayo

Directions:

- First, you will want to heat your oven to 400 degrees. As the oven warms up, take your sweet potato and toss it in oil. When this step is complete, place the diced sweet potato pieces in a single layer on a baking sheet. Once this is done, pop the sheet into the oven and cook for about twenty minutes. Halfway through, flip the pieces over to assure the sweet potato cooks all the way through. When this is done, remove the sheet from the oven and allow the sweet potato to cool down slightly.
- Next, you will want to get out your food processor. When you are ready, add in the beans, sweet potatoes, breadcrumbs, cayenne, cumin, soy sauce, garlic, and onion pieces. Once in place, begin to pulse the ingredients together until you have a finely chopped mixture. As you do this, season the "dough" with pepper and salt as desired. Now, shape the dough into four patties.
- When your patties are formed, begin to heat a large skillet over medium heat. As the pan warms up, place your oil and then grill each side of your patties. Typically, this will take five to six minutes on each side. You will know the burger is cooked through when it is browned on each side.
- All you need to do now is assemble your burger! If you want, try baking the pineapple rings—three minutes on each side should do the trick!
- Top your burger with lettuce, tomato, and vegan mayo for some extra flavor.

34. *Cheesy Mac and Cheese*

Course: Lunch/Dinner

Prep Time: 5 minutes

Cook Time: 30minutes

Total Time: 35 minutes

Servings: 6

Ingredients:

- Tahini (1 T.)
- Turmeric (.50 t.)
- Paprika (.50 t.)
- Dry Mustard (.50 t.)
- Garlic Puree (.50 t.)
- Salt (1 t.)
- Lemon Juice (1 T.)
- Corn Starch (3 T.)
- Nutritional Yeast (.75 C.)
- Almond Milk (1 C.)
- Water (1.25 C.)
- Pasta (1 Lb.)
- Black Pepper (.25 t.)

Directions:

- To start off, you will want to prepare your pasta according to the directions that are provided on the side of the box.

- As the pasta is cooking, you will want to include the rest of the ingredients from the list above into a blender and blend until smooth. Typically, this will take thirty to sixty seconds.
- When your pasta is ready, place it in a pot and pour the sauce of the top. Once everything is in place, go ahead and turn the heat to low or medium. As the pot begins to warm up, stir everything together frequently. It will take the sauce anywhere from five to ten minutes to thicken properly. If you are looking to get more vegetables into your day, feel free to add red bell pepper, spinach, or any of your favorite vegetables for some extra flavor.

35.   *Black Bean Meatloaf*

Course: Lunch/Dinner

Prep Time: 10 minutes

Cook Time: 55 minutes

Total Time: 65 minutes

Servings: 4

Ingredients:

- Chopped Red Bell Pepper (1)
- Quick Oats (1.50 C.)
- Black Beans (2 Cans)
- Ketchup (3 T.)
- Cumin (1 t.)
- Liquid Aminos (1 T.)
- Minced Garlic (1)
- Minced Onion (1)
- Chopped Carrot (1)
- Black Pepper (.25 t.)

Directions:

- First, you will want to heat your oven to 350 degrees. While the oven warms up, you can begin preparing your dinner.
- Over medium heat, place a medium sized pan and begin to sauté your onions. You can use water or oil to complete this step. As the

onion turns translucent, add in your carrot pieces, pepper, and the garlic. You will want to cook these ingredients for six to eight minutes. By the end, the carrots and pepper should be nice and soft.

- Next, you will want to get out a large bowl. In this bowl, carefully combine the oats, black beans, and all of the seasonings from the list above. Once these are in place, add in the vegetables you just cooked and mash everything together. Combine all of the ingredients well but not enough to make the mixture mushy. If the ingredients are too hard to form a "dough," add water or moist oats to help hold everything together.

- When your dough is ready, you can pour it into a lined loaf pan. Once in place, pop the dish into your heated oven for about thirty minutes. By the end, the edges should develop a nice, browned crust. At this point, you will want to remove the dish from the oven and allow it to cool for a bit.

- Serve with your favorite vegetable side!

36. *Taco Pasta Bowl*

Course: Lunch/Dinner

Prep Time: 5 minutes

Cook Time: 30 minutes

Total Time: 35 minutes

Servings: 4

Ingredients:

- Black Beans (1 Can)
- Corn (1 C.)
- Diced Onion (.50 C.)
- Salsa (1 Jar)
- Pasta (1 Box)
- Cumin (.25 t.)
- Chili Powder (2 T.)

Directions:

- To start, please cook the pasta of your choice according to the directions provided on the box. Once this step is complete, you can drain the water and set the pasta to the side.
- Next, you will want to take a medium pan and place it over medium to high heat. Add one tablespoon of your oil and bring it to sizzle.

Once the oil is hot, place your onion and cook for three to five minutes. By the end, the onion should be soft.

- At this point, you will add in the beans, corn, salsa, and spices. I have chosen to use chili powder and cumin, but you can spice your dish however you would like!
- Last, you will pour your sauce over your pasta and enjoy!

37. *Avocado Pasta*

Course: Lunch/Dinner

Prep Time: 5 minutes

Cook Time: 15 minutes

Total Time: 20 minutes

Servings: 4

Ingredients:

- Corn (.50 C.)
- Cherry Tomatoes (1 C.)
- Olive Oil (.33 C.)
- Black Pepper (.25 t.)
- Salt (.25 t.)
- Lemon Juice (2 T.)
- Garlic Cloves (2)
- Basil Leaves (.50 C.)
- Avocados (2)
- Spaghetti (12 Oz.)

Directions:

- To begin this easy recipe, you will first want to cook your pasta. You will want to do this step according to the directions provided on the pasta's package. Once the pasta is cooked through, drain the water and place the pasta to the side.

- As the pasta is cooking, you can begin to make your avocado sauce. To do this, you will be placing the lemon juice, garlic, basil, and pitted avocados into a food processor. When everything is in place, go ahead and season the ingredients with salt and pepper according to your own taste. As you run the processor, carefully add the olive oil until you achieve a creamy texture for your sauce.
- Now, take a large bowl and place your pasta. Gently pour the sauce over the top and stir everything together. As a final touch, add in the corn and cherry tomatoes. Serve immediately and enjoy your dinner!

à

38.   *Orzo and Broccoli*

Course: Lunch/Dinner

Prep Time: 5 minutes

Cook Time: 20 minutes

Total Time: 25 minutes

Servings: 3

Ingredients:

- Olive Oil (3 t.)
- Smashed Garlic Cloves (4)
- Broccoli Florets (2 C.)
- Orzo Pasta (4.50 Oz.)
- Salt (.25 t.)
- Pepper (.25 t.)

Directions:

- Start off by preparing your broccoli. You can do this by trimming the stems off and slicing the broccoli into small, bite-size pieces. If you want, go ahead and season with salt.
- Next, you will want to steam your broccoli over a little bit of water until it is cooked through. Once the broccoli is cooked, chop it up into even smaller pieces.

- When the broccoli is done, cook your pasta according to the directions provided on the box. Once this is done, drain the water and then place the pasta back into the pot.
- With the pasta and broccoli done, place it back into the pot with the garlic. Stir everything together well and cook until the garlic turns a nice golden color. Be sure to stir everything to combine your meal well. Serve warm and enjoy a simple dinner!

39. *Garlic Zucchini and Lentils*

Course: Lunch/Dinner

Prep Time: 5 minutes

Cook Time: 20 minutes

Total Time: 25 minutes

Servings: 4

Ingredients:

- Zucchini (4)
- Ground Coriander (1 T.)
- Ground Cumin (1 T.)
- Onion (1)
- Cumin Seeds (1 t.)
- Crushed Garlic Cloves (6)
- Olive Oil (2 T.)
- Water (4 C.)
- Salt (2 t.)
- Ground Turmeric (.50 t.)
- Lentils (1 C.)
- Coriander (2 T.)
- Paprika (.50 t.)

Directions:

- To begin, you will want to take a large saucepan and place it over medium heat. As the pan heats up, add in the water, lentils, salt, and turmeric. Bring the ingredients to a boil and then reduce the heat. When you have completed this step, carefully cover the pan and cook the lentils for fifteen to twenty minutes. By the end, the lentils should be fluffy, and all the liquid will be gone. If the lentils are cooked through, transfer them to a serving bowl and place to the side.

- Next, you will take another saucepan and place it over medium heat. As the pan warms up, add in the olive oil and garlic. Sauté the garlic for two minutes or until it becomes a nice golden color. At this point, add in the chopped zucchini, onion, and your cumin seeds. Go ahead and cook all of these ingredients for five minutes, or until the zucchini and onion are soft. Finally, add in the cumin and ground coriander. Be sure to stir everything together well to assure even coating of the spices.

- Last, you are going to divide the lentils into serving bowls and top with the spiced vegetables. For extra flavor, try adding fresh coriander leaves. It is also delicious with a side of warm Indian bread or rice.

40.   *Vegetable Shepherd's Pie*

Course: Lunch/Dinner

Prep Time: 15 minutes

Cook Time: 55 minutes

Total Time: 70 minutes

Servings: 6

Ingredients:

- Vegan Butter (4 T.)
- Gold Potatoes (3 Lbs.)
- Mixed Frozen Vegetables (10 Oz.)
- Fresh Thyme (2 t.)
- Vegetable Stock (4 C.)
- Green Lentils (1.50 C.)
- Garlic (2)
- Diced Onion (1)
- Salt (.25 t.)
- Pepper (.25 t.)

Directions:

- To begin, we will prepare the potatoes. While I enjoy the Gold Potatoes, you can use any of your likings. When you have chosen your potatoes, slice them in half and then bring them to a boil over high heat. Once the potatoes are in place, add some salt and cook for thirty minutes. By the end, the skin should come off fairly easily. When they are done, drain the water and place back into a mixing bowl.
- When the potatoes are in your mixing bowl, you will want to use a masher to begin breaking the potato apart. If you would like, use some vegan butter to make a smoother mashed potato. At this point, you will also want to add pepper and salt according to taste. Once this step is complete, place the potatoes to the side.

- Now, you will want to heat your oven to 425 degrees. As the oven heats up, grease up a baking dish and then set it to the side.
- Next, you will be taking a large saucepan and placing it over medium heat. Once the pan is warmed up, add in your olive oil, garlic, and onions. Cook these onions until they are caramelized and slightly brown. Typically, this will take about five minutes.
- When the onions are done, you can add your stock and lentils into the pan. Be sure to give the ingredients a good stir and then add in the salt, pepper, and thyme. As the stock begins to boil, reduce your heat to low and allowing everything to simmer. Now, you will want to cook everything in this pan for about forty minutes. Within the last ten minutes, add in your frozen veggies and allow them to cook through.
- Once the vegetable mix is cooked through, carefully transfer the ingredients into the baking dish that you prepared a bit earlier. At this point, you can add any extra seasonings you desire. When everything is settled, top the dish with the mashed potatoes and smooth it down with a fork or a spoon.
- Next, you will place the baking dish on a baking sheet in the case of overflow. When you are ready, pop the dish into the oven for about fifteen minutes. When the dish is cooked through, the mashed potatoes will begin to turn a light brown color. Once you have achieved this, remove the dish from the oven, allow to cool slightly, and enjoy!

SIDE DISH

41.   *Roasted Green Beans*

Course: Side Dish

Prep Time: 5 minutes

Cook Time: 20 minutes

Total Time: 25 minutes

Servings: 6

Ingredients

- 2 pounds' green beans
- 2 tbsp. olive oil
- 1 tsp. kosher salt
- ½ tsp. ground pepper, fresh

Directions

- Preheat your oven at 400F/200 C.
- Wash and rinse the green beans (make sure that the beans are neat, dry well).
- Arrange the green beans on a jelly roll pan & drizzle olive oil over it.
- Sprinkle with pepper and salt to taste.

- Coat the beans evenly using your hands and then spread the beans out into one layer.
- Roast until beans are somewhat shriveled and fairly brown in the spots, approximately half an hour; don't forget to turn the beans after every 10 to 15 minutes.
- Serve at room temperature or hot.

42.   *Roasted Garlic & Broccoli*

Course: Side Dish

Prep Time: 5 minutes

Cook Time: 30 minutes

Total Time: 35 minutes

Servings: 4

Ingredients

- 9 cups broccoli florets
- 12 oz. garlic, peeled & cloves separated (approximately 3 heads)
- 2 tbsp. soy sauce
- 1 tsp. sesame oil
- 2 tsp. olive oil

Directions

- Lightly oil a baking pan (preferably 8-10" square).
- Put olive oil in the pan & mix with the garlic cloves.
- Bake at 475F /245C approximately 20 minutes; until the garlic starts becoming brown (don't overdo it).

103

- Bring a pot (preferably large) of water to boil, while the garlic is still roasting.
- Add the broccoli to the water, the moment it starts boiling & cook approximately 5 minutes (just heat the broccoli and ensure it's still very crisp).
- Drain and then put it in cold water. Drain and repeat the process with broccoli.
- Mix the sesame oil & soy sauce in a shallow bowl and then add the mixture to the garlic & stir.
- Put this mixture over the broccoli & toss well.

43.   *Hot Potato Curry*

Course: Side Dish

Prep Time: 5 minutes

Cook Time: 55 minutes

Total Time: 60 minutes

Servings: 4

Ingredients:

- Coconut Milk (14 Oz.)
- Peas (15 Oz)
- Garbanzo Beans (15 Oz.)
- Diced Tomatoes (14.5 Oz.)
- Salt (2 t.)
- Minced Ginger Root (1)
- Garam Masala (4 t.)
- Curry Powder (4 t.)
- Cayenne Pepper (1.50 t.)
- Ground Cumin (2 t.)
- Minced Garlic (3)
- Diced Yellow Onion (1)
- Vegetable Oil (2 T.)
- Cubed Potatoes (4)

Directions:

- To start, you will want to cook your potatoes. All you need to do is bring a pot of water over high heat until the water begins to boil. When the water begins to boil, reduce the heat and place a cover over the pot. Simmer the potatoes in the water for about fifteen minutes and then drain the water.

- As the potatoes are cooking, you will want to bring a large skillet over medium heat. As the pan begins to warm up, place your vegetable oil and onion. Cook the onion for five minutes or until it becomes soft. Now, add in the salt, ginger, garam masala, curry powder, cayenne pepper, cumin, and the garlic. At this point, you will want to cook all of these ingredients for two or three minutes.

- Once the ingredients are warmed through, add in the cooked potatoes, peas, tomatoes, and the garbanzo beans. When these are all in place, carefully pour in the coconut milk and allow the pan to come to a simmer. Simmer this dish for five to ten minutes and then remove from heat.

...in the end.

It's true, being vegan means:

- saving the environment
- not killing animals
- taking care of your body
- eating in a healthy and natural way

but this does not mean having to give up the pleasure of eating.

Now you know how delicious your vegan diet can be!

EASY VEGAN COOKBOOK
FOR BEGINNERS

CPSIA information can be obtained
at www.ICGtesting.com
Printed in the USA
LVHW062110090421
684056LV00004B/569

9 781801 696142